SCOTT RUSSELL HILL is Austr
paranormal and spiritual pheno
World's Most Accurate Psychic!" ᴛ̲ᴇ ꜱᴛᴀ̲ʀ̲ᴇ̲ᴅ̲ ᴵ̲ꜰ̲ ᴛ̲ᴇ̲
and New Zealand versions of the popular psychic detective
show SENSING MURDER.

PSYCHIC DETECTIVE

SCOTT RUSSELL HILL

This is Book #4 of the
CAUGHT BETWEEN TWO WORLDS
Series of books

Also by Scott Russell Hill

CAUGHT BETWEEN TWO WORLDS
PSYCHIC
AWAKENING
GRATEFUL

scottrussellhill.com

National Library of Australia
Cataloguing-in-publication data:
Hill, Scott
Caught Between Two Worlds
ISBN 1534723951 / 9781534723955
1. Hill, Scott 2. Prophecies (Occultism)
3. Prophets – Biography

Typeset by Garron Publishing, Adelaide
Printed in Australia by On-Demand, Melbourne

"Clues to every case are in *every* case!"

From the Author

Originally released in 2006, *Psychic Detective* was primarily about my time working as a psychic detective on TV's *Sensing Murder*. One of the cases I worked on was Mersina Halvagis. A man has since been found guilty of her murder, and that update is included in this revised edition.

Separate to my *Sensing Murder* cases was my private investigations into missing Sunshine Coast boy Daniel Morcombe, and my friends the Beaumont children.

In 2011 a man was charged with Daniel's murder, and many details about the case were made public by police. It's interesting now to look back at what I wrote about Daniel in the original *Psychic Detective*.

How much did I get right or wrong?
You'll read that for yourself.
My further involvement in 2013 with the Beaumont children case is also included in the revised edition of *Psychic Detective*.

Enjoy!

Scott Russell Hill

May 2015

Foreword

It's a hot summer day in a quietly respectable suburban street. Bright flowers bloom in neat front yards, and the atmosphere is hushed, although the noise and bustle of Adelaide's Glenelg Beach are only minutes away. Nothing remarkable could ever have happened here, or so it seems. And then psychic Scott Russell Hill parks his car, winds down the window, and gestures down a garden path.

"Take a look down there beside the house. See where those pot plants are placed? That's the area where I feel the Beaumont children were taken, just by the boundary fence."

I suppress a shudder. It's been decades since the three Beaumont children disappeared without a trace at Glenelg, sparking one of Australia's most tragic and intriguing mysteries. And now Scott is telling me he knows what happened to them.

It sounds incredible. How could he have cracked a case that's baffled some of this country's finest detectives for so long? How could he have seen the glowing ghost of little Grant, still wearing his bathers, in the Beaumonts' lounge room several years after they disappeared? And yet …

During the time I've known and worked with Scott on numerous stories for *Woman's Day* magazine, or watched his uncanny psychic detective skills on TV's *Sensing Murder*, I've learned to take him seriously.

I've heard tapes from his Adelaide radio show that prove he foretold Princess Diana's death, and the 9/11 terrorist attacks down to the month, years before they happened. Somehow, Scott pinpointed that the Princess would be killed in Paris before her 40th birthday. Somehow he prophesied that the World Trade Centre would be struck from the air, with catastrophic results. And those are just a couple of examples of the mysterious power that descended on Scott following a near-death experience when he drowned as a child.

It sounds spooky, and it is, but there's nothing ethereal about him in person. Down-to-earth Scott doesn't waft around trailing Indian scarves reeking of patchouli oil, or make airy-fairy utterances. He's a big, burly bloke with the sort of deep brown voice that makes him a natural as a radio announcer, which is where he started out. On one hand he has a wickedly hilarious, irreverent, sense of humour. On the other hand he is solidly grounded and teaches karate several times a week - when he's not giving readings to his many clients, some of them world-famous celebrities. But their secrets are safe with Scott, who recognises that his extraordinary gift brings great responsibilities in its wake. Unravelling the truth of unsolved murders – and bringing closure to grief-stricken families - is just one of them.

I still can't come close to explaining how Scott does what he does. He can't fully explain it either. But having played Dr Watson to his Sherlock Holmes for close to a decade, I'm sure there's something going on. Whether you're a believer or not, I guarantee that you'll be moved and intrigued by the remarkable casebook of Scott Russell Hill, Psychic Detective.

Jenny Brown - Woman's Day

Introduction

The first time I saw her was on one of those stormy winter's nights when any person with the slightest degree of sanity was home tucked up safe and warm in bed. I was returning home from a birthday party and driving along the freeway through the Adelaide Hills in the early hours of the morning, when unexpectedly up ahead I thought I could see a person standing on the side of the freeway in the drizzling rain, wind and fog.

'What the hell is that?' I said out loud. 'It looks like a little girl!' Were my eyes playing tricks on me? I squinted for a better look as my car approached its headlights lighting up the scene. Sure enough, it *was* a little girl! What was she doing out here alone at this hour in the middle of such a stormy night? I passed the little girl as I slowed my car to a complete stop in the freeway's emergency lane. Leaving the engine idling I opened the driver's door and the hands of winter embraced me. Away from the warmth inside my car the sudden temperature drop made me shiver, and I folded my arms across my chest in a vain attempt to protect myself from the cold. With my face now wet from the drizzling rain, I slowly walked towards the little girl, as I didn't want to make any quick movement that would scare her. She looked about ten-years-old. Her straight, fair hair hung to just below her shoulders, and she wore a knee-length pink pinafore dress with a white blouse underneath.

'Are you lost sweetheart?' I called out as I approached her.

She didn't answer, nor did her calm demeanour change, even though I thought she might be nervous or apprehensive. As I got closer, I noticed that even though it was raining, she wasn't wet. Her hair looked as shiny and clean as if she was walking in bright sunshine. I got to within three metres of her before I noticed a shimmering blue light around her, the light that I always see surrounding people when they're in spirit or from "the other side". She was a ghost! The realisation stopped me in my tracks! Before I'd gotten close enough to tell the difference, the little girl had looked just like a normal everyday living person!

I shivered again and crossed my folded arms tighter against my chest. My teeth began to chatter as we stood facing each other. I wasn't scared or nervous, but I was cold, so cold that I decided to cut to the chase!

'Look,' I said in a friendly but firm tone. 'I'm freezing! So if you've got something to say or you need my help, now would be a good time to tell me.'

The little girl took a couple of steps towards me and I waited for her to say something. But she didn't. She just smiled, and faded from view, leaving me standing on the side of the freeway.

'Well that's just bloody marvellous!' I sarcastically muttered, shivering and soaked to the skin.

Headlights from an approaching car came into view and I high-tailed it to my car, where back inside once again I turned the heating up so that my body, hands and face would defrost. I took off my rain-soaked shirt and put on a dry jacket that I'd brought with me. Lined with lamb's wool, the jacket instantly cocooned me in warmth.

The car whose headlights I'd seen approaching sped past and disappeared around a curve in the freeway just ahead. I took one last glance behind me to where the little girl in the pink dress had been standing, and there was nothing there now but swirling fog. So with no other oncoming traffic in sight, I steered my car back onto the freeway and was on my way again.

Seeing the little girl and knowing that she was a ghost didn't faze me at all. Since my near-death-experience when I drowned as a seven-year-old, I'd seen plenty of ghosts over the years and took the reality of their existence in my stride. The spirit world and the physical world mix and mingle all the time, we coexist with each other, so seeing her wasn't an issue. As the fog thickened and the rain fell in a sudden, heavier downpour, I put my car's windscreen wipers on double speed, and pondered the only question that was on my mind.

Who was she?

Chapter 1

DEAL

'No.'

'Why not?'

'No.'

'I think you'd be a great asset to the show.'

'Well I appreciate that but like I told you before, Lisa. I'm just not interested!'

Lisa was a segment producer and researcher for a new psychic TV show called *Sensing Murder*. In doing preliminary research and compiling a list of psychics who could possibly take part, I'd come highly recommended to Lisa through some mutual friends in the TV industry. Lisa had then done her homework by resourcing magazine and newspaper articles about me, and checking out my website. She was on the phone from Melbourne for a second attempt at trying to convince me to take part in *Sensing Murder*. Her first attempt had been a year earlier when the show was with Channel Seven. It was now with Channel Ten.

Part of me was really interested in working on *Sensing Murder*. I was always up for a new challenge. In my daily work of doing readings I'd regularly come across people who were grief stricken because they'd lost a loved one in tragic circumstances such as murder, suicide, or a car crash. So as my role had always been to help people through those difficult times, I now had a problem grasping the idea of going to the other side of the coin and possibly upsetting the family and friends of a murder victim by bringing up memories of the unsolved case again. The only way I'd feel comfortable was if I definitely knew that I could come up with new information to help solve the case, but as I wasn't greatly experienced specifically in the psychic detective field, I wasn't sure that I could do that.

'Can I ask why you're saying no?' Lisa enquired.

Rather than go into detail of how I *really* felt, I gave a simple response. 'Because working on murder cases really isn't my thing.'

'But Scott, last time we spoke you told me that you were trying to solve the riddle of the missing Beaumont children.'

'I still am.'

'And the Beaumont children have been missing for what, thirty years?'

'Almost forty.'

'Isn't that classed as a murder case?'

'Of course,' I said, 'but the Beaumont children is different. I'm working on that case in my own time at my own pace for personal reasons!'

'Which are?'

'Well, I knew the Beaumont children when I was a kid. They were my friends.'

Lisa remained quiet for a few moments after I revealed my connection to the Beaumont children. She hadn't been expecting that.

'I can understand you wanting to try and solve the case then,' she finally said.

'Aside from that,' I added, 'my psychic abilities are more about empowering people, helping them to make more informed choices in their lives and understand their spirituality better. That's what I enjoy doing the most.'

'Okay, I accept that,' said Lisa, but what about when you predicted the September 11 attack, Princess Diana's accident in Paris, and the Bali Bombings. Isn't making predictions a specialty area too?'

'What's your point?' I asked.

'Well, Scott. From where I'm standing you obviously specialise in a *lot* of things on a spiritual level! I'd say you have a tremendous gift! What if solving murder cases is part of that gift?'

'Lisa, I don't want to upset people.'

'Neither do we,' Lisa said. 'Trust me. How you're feeling, we feel too. But the reality is that the greatest upset has already been done! A loved one has been murdered! Sure, stirring the pot by featuring unsolved cases on *Sensing Murder* might not be popular with everyone connected to the victim, but the crime isn't going to go away just because we don't feature it on the show. We hope through what we're doing on *Sensing Murder* that we can bring some closure to the victim's family and friends.'

I felt better when Lisa told me that because she confirmed that *Sensing Murder* was being done for all the right reasons. And yes, not doing a case wouldn't make it go away. I agreed with that. And I also agreed that the loved ones were already upset. But because of my connection to the Beaumont children I also knew what it felt like to have so many unanswered questions. The unknown part just ate me alive; it was always in the back of my mind. And I also know first-hand that ignoring the situation doesn't make it go away. I felt the only thing that could ultimately help ease the pain surrounding the Beaumont Case were new clues that could lead to some form of closure. That's what I wanted for the Beaumont parents, and that's what I'd want for the family and friends connected to the cases featured on *Sensing Murder* if I did the show.

'Do you have the support of the families in all the cases?' I asked.

'Not all of them,' Lisa answered. 'Some aren't keen to keep publicly living the memory. And we understand that. Other families and friends are working with us every step of the way. We've become quite close to them.'

'Will you still do the cases where the families aren't involved?'

'Absolutely. Each case is a matter of public record. If we don't bring the case up again, someone else will in some shape or form. Again, our most important reason for doing *Sensing Murder* is to gather enough new evidence so that each case can be solved.' There was a pause as Lisa took a thoughtful breath after which she cut to the bottom line. 'Scott. We *really* want you for the show.'

'Would I still have to try and solve the case in a day?' I asked.

'Yes.'

'And I wouldn't be told what the case is? Not a single clue?'

'That's right,' Lisa confirmed. 'That's the format of the show. The psychics are told nothing!'

'Well,' I said, 'that makes things incredibly difficult! Wouldn't it save a lot of time and trouble if you told me what the case was?'

'Yes, it probably would,' agreed Lisa. 'But a big part of the *Sensing Murder* format is that the psychics must use their talents to figure out what the case is. Scott, we believe in you so much that we're willing to pay you whether you come up with anything or not!'

'When is filming scheduled to start?' I asked.

'In three weeks.'

'If I did agree where do we go from here?' I asked.

'Well I'd still like you to audition, get you on camera, show you photos of our test cases and see what you come up with, and see what you look like on camera.'

'When do you want that to happen?'

'Next week. Deal?'

'Well,' I said. 'I'll have to move a few things around in my diary, but deal.'

I hung up the phone from Lisa, made a coffee and went outside to clear my head. It was a sunny, crisp, autumn afternoon. I sat on the back step of my house and watched a starling decide whether it wanted to tackle the remnants of an old loaf of bread that I'd scattered outside the previous day. The starling tapped at the dried out bread with its beak a few times, figured that a better menu could be found elsewhere, and flew away. Rays of sunshine trickled down through tree branches and across my face. Yes, the time constraints and secrecy surrounding the filming of *Sensing Murder* were major issues I'd have to deal with. And who knows. Maybe I'd even pick up a few new psychic skills by having to work under such pressure! Wouldn't surprise me if I did. Hmm, there could be some interesting times ahead!

"Interesting", of course, would turn out to be an understatement.

"Life-altering" would be more accurate!

Chapter 2

AUDITION

A week later, the day of my audition arrived. It was scheduled for 4.00 pm at a hotel in the city. I found a park easily and arrived at the hotel right on time. I walked across shiny polished tiles to the front desk.

'Whereabouts are the auditions for *Sensing Murder* being held I asked the receptionist.

She returned a perplexed look, which is never a good sign.

'The auditions for what?'

'*Sensing Murder,*' I repeated.

'Hmm,' she said thoughtfully. 'To be honest, I haven't a clue what you're talking about. Auditions, you say?'

'Yeah. For a TV show.'

'Just a minute,' smiled the receptionist, and she scanned a guest list. After a few moments a noticeable scowl appeared on her face and she shook her head. 'Not that I can see.'

I glanced at a large clock on the wall. Now I was late for my audition. But I'd double-checked the hotel name. This was definitely the one I'd been told to go to! With other people banking up behind me I thanked the receptionist and walked out into the bustling city street. Maybe they've mixed up the hotels, I thought. A few new buildings had sprung up in the past couple of years, and as I rarely ventured into the city I was unfamiliar with them all, but maybe one of them was the correct hotel and there'd been a mix up.

So off I went to investigate, and sure enough just around the corner was a brand new hotel, which had a name eerily similar to the one I'd just been to, and this time at the reception desk I had success!

'Go to room 1214,' I was told. 'The lifts are just over there.'

As I entered the lift I jokingly thought that being told the wrong hotel and then finding the right one should be enough to get me on *Sensing Murder* without the audition! I wondered if the hotel mistake had been made on purpose to test me out!

The lady handling the auditions was Tricia, and she was very happy that I finally made it, and was most sympathetic to my plight about being given the wrong hotel name.

'It wasn't a deliberate "mistake" Tricia?' I asked good-humouredly.

'Not at all,' she told me. 'It was definitely a genuine mix-up.'

That matter out the way, Tricia then asked me to take a seat in front of a camera and to make myself comfortable. She pressed the record button.

'Now look, Scott,' she said, 'I know you prefer to work from dates of birth and not photos, but this is purely so that we can see what you look like on camera.'

'No problem.'

'Why is that by the way?' Tricia asked.

'I'm sorry?'

'Why do you prefer to work from dates of birth?'

'Well …'

'Or,' she interrupted, 'perhaps a better way of asking the question would be *how* do you work from dates of birth?'

'Well, I guess the easiest way to explain it is that the numbers talk to me. For me a date of birth is a person's blueprint of why they're here and what makes them tick; it reveals their positive and negative behaviour, and good and bad time cycles. When I've got a person's date of birth I know exactly what and *who* I'm dealing with because the numbers don't lie. Through all societies, languages and cultures, numbers are the universal language.'

'Is it something you've learnt?' Tricia concluded.

'No, it's just something I do. Some people tune in through candles, or stones or crystals or cards. I prefer numbers.'

'So numerology in other words?' Tricia said.

'To a point,' I said, 'but a lot of the information I gain is *beyond* numerology. For me a date of birth is also a gateway to a psychic level where all kinds of different information from spirit becomes available. I actually tried to teach the way I do numerology to a group of psychologists once. They were looking for some added insight into human behaviour. Anyway, in a frustrating moment when they couldn't pick up on certain things like I did, one of them pointed out that while I *could* teach them basic skills, I *couldn't* teach them what *I* picked up on intuitively; and that for as simple as I made working from dates of birth look, it was obviously a far more complex process than even I imagined.'

'So,' Tricia pondered, 'can you not work from photos at all?'

'It's not that I can't,' I explained. 'I just don't feel comfortable working from photos. I don't feel in my element.'

'Well now that you've told me that I almost feel stupid showing you these photos,' Tricia said, referring to the two she was holding.

'Don't worry about it,' I smiled. 'It's just so I'll be doing something on camera, right?'

'Tricia nodded. 'Right.'

'Hand them over then,' I said. 'And,' I added as a psychic impression came to mind, 'before I look at them can I just say that these *weren't* the photos that Lisa originally intended to show me!' I looked down the lens of the camera. 'Lisa!' I said cheekily, 'What was the original case you were going to audition me on?'

Lisa would later confirm that a British case was originally selected as an audition photo. The case was that of two-year-old James Bulger, who in 1993 was led away from a shopping mall by two ten-year-old boys, and murdered. But that case was discarded from the audition process after it was felt it might be too well known!

I shifted in my chair and got comfortable.
'Okay,' I said, 'Let's get down to business!'
The first photo was an old black and white image of three children, two girls and a boy.

Audition Photo 1

It looked similar in vintage and age to the missing Beaumont children. It wasn't them, but it reminded me of them, which clouded my thinking. I made a comment about that similarity and moved onto the next photo, which was in colour. It was of a very pretty teenage girl.

Audition Photo 2

I looked at the photo for about ten seconds.

'I don't pick up anything, Tricia,' I finally said.

'Nothing?'

'Nope. It's not always instant with me. Just out of interest do you have her date of birth?'

Tricia flicked through a folder of notes. 'You know something, Scott?' she said. 'I've got heaps of photos, but no dates of birth.'

'Well don't worry,' I said as I handed back the photo. 'When something comes to mind, I'll let you know, okay?'

'When do you think that might be? Tricia asked.

'That I pick up on something?' She nodded. 'Well, it could be when I'm going out the door, when I'm going down in the lift, when I'm washing the dishes, or when I'm driving my car. It could be in one hour, one day or a week. I don't know when Tricia. Hopefully it won't be too long. It depends on how easily I receive some psychic impressions from the other side.

'Tricia handed me her card. 'Well call me as soon as you get anything, okay?'

'Absolutely!'

I dashed home from the hotel, put my karate uniform on, and went to class. As the class progressed I became distracted by images and thoughts surrounding the teenage girl in the photo; they appeared over and over in my mind like a scene out of a movie playing on an endless loop. I kept seeing the girl, a thin metal bar, and a house that friends of mine had bought in Bryan, Ohio, USA, a two-storey family place. I'd assumed that the test case would be Australian, but was I seeing my friend's house in Ohio because the case was American? Perhaps the girl was from Ohio. Hmm, or maybe she'd moved to Australia from America? Whatever the situation was, I felt that the *Sensing Murder* producers were trying to make the audition process as difficult as possible!

In between concentrating on throwing front and spinning kicks at karate, I mentally placed the girl's photo on a map of Australia, moving her image from state to state in my mind until I got a stronger energy on which state she was from. I didn't get energy from *any* state in Australia, just the persistent image of my friend's house in Ohio. If the girl was from, or lived in Australia, then her image would match up to one of the states or cities on the map that I was visualising. But there was no match. This is an American case, I thought. It has to be! And the longer the spiritual symbols and images persisted, the more my theory was supported.

When karate finished just after 9pm I called Tricia on her mobile as I was driving home. She'd just returned to Melbourne after flying back from my audition.

'I'm sorry to call you this late, Tricia,' I said, 'but there's a couple of things I'd like to run past you. If I'm wrong, I'm wrong. But it's worth a try, right?'

'Absolutely!' she said, 'I'm glad you've called. What do you want to run past me?'

I took a deep breath, ready to give it my best shot. 'Okay, well, the girl in the colour photo. I can't completely match the energy that's coming from her photo to the energy of Australia. She wouldn't happen to be from America by any chance?'

There was a short silence on Tricia's end of the phone. 'Yes she would,' Tricia finally answered.

'Then hers is an American case, not an Australian one. Correct?'

'Correct.'

'Is she from Ohio?'

'No.'

'Does the name Bryan or Brian have something to do with the case?'

'Not that I know of.'

'Not to worry,' I said. 'Now that you've told me that she's from America the symbols and images that I'm seeing are matching up better! I'm getting the name Marcia, like Marcia in *The Brady Bunch*. Is Marcia the name of this girl?'

'I can see what you're picking up on. You're close,' Tricia confirmed.

Close? I quickly tried to come up with an alternative name. I almost said Marcie, but I was sure the girl's name ended with an "uh" sound rather than an "ee". As I couldn't come up with another name right at that moment, I continued with my questions.

'Was she attacked or bashed with something metal like a steel pole?'

'Yes.'

'Was she attacked by a man who she knew quite well?

'Indeed she was. Scott, you've basically nailed the case. That's exactly what we were hoping you'd be able to do. You're only slightly off on the name. Do you have any further thoughts on that?'

'No,' I answered. 'My mind's stuck on Marcia.'

'Well Scott,' Tricia said, 'it's actually Martha!'

Martha Moxley was fifteen-years-old when she died in 1975 in wealthy Greenwich, Connecticut, USA. It took until 2002 to convict her neighbour, Michael Skakel of bludgeoning Martha to death with a golf club when he was also fifteen-years-old. Skakel's older brother Thomas was an early suspect because he was the last person to be seen with Martha, but investigators later focused on Michael because of reports of incriminating statements he had made over the years. Some of Michael Skakel's friends and classmates testified that he was romantically interested in Martha and was jealous because Thomas was competing for her affections.

When Lisa and I next spoke by phone, she confirmed that I'd passed the audition.

'I'm so glad to have you on board!' she told me. 'As you discovered with the Martha case, the audition parameters were that the photos could be of any case, from any year, from anywhere in the world! We did that deliberately, just in case the auditioning psychics decided to jump on the Internet and try and do some research beforehand! It's certainly sorted out the would-be-could-be's from the real thing! In recent months we've auditioned over 100 psychics and only five, including you, were able to come up with consistent, accurate information. Are you surprised that you did?' Lisa asked.

'Um, surprised? No,' I said. 'Nothing about the spiritual world ever surprises me. I'd say I'm more relieved! The families of the victims have been through enough already. I didn't want to add to their grief by raising their hopes and then not coming up with anything. Now that I know the spirits *will* talk to me, I can get on with the job! So, what happens now?' I asked.

'Well, Scott, you and I need to agree on some dates when you can start filming. I'll tell you what timeframe we have according to our schedule, and you can tell me if that suits you. I also need to tell you that with regard to all the cases, your first stop will be Melbourne but you may not stay in Melbourne. You could well stop off here and then fly on to another location anywhere in Australia, so be prepared! And remember Scott; your role on *Sensing Murder* is to come up with new leads, not just to say what's already public knowledge. You have to come up with new information that our private investigators can check out and validate!'

'I'll do my best,' I said.

The success I'd had tuning into the Martha Moxley case pushed aside any remaining hesitation I had in doing *Sensing Murder*. I felt confident and assured, and couldn't wait to begin filming!

Chapter 3

THE LITTLE GIRL

With filming scheduled to begin a couple of weeks later, I got on with my day-to-day routine, and didn't place extra pressure on myself to receive messages from the other side. I knew that the spirits would talk to me if they wanted to.

One night around midnight, I remembered that I hadn't checked the letterbox, so I wandered outside and collected two letters and some junk mail. I looked up at the stars and saw the Southern Cross, and then noticed a satellite passing overhead. Hmm, I thought. Whether it's on *this* side, or the *other* side, there's *always* someone watching us! I tracked the satellite across the sky until it disappeared, and then turned to walk back along the driveway towards my house, when I saw the little girl in the pink dress. She was standing on the porch by the front door surrounded by shimmering, blue light, and looked just as she had when I saw her on the freeway that stormy night. Her sudden appearance startled me.

'Hello,' I said.

The little girl didn't move or speak. She seemed quite comfortable just to stand on the front porch and observe me.

'Would you like to tell me your name?' I asked, 'because I'd really like to know who you are.'

She didn't respond, so I tried another approach. 'I'm Scott. Is there something you want to tell me?'

With that question she stepped off the porch and faded from view. Knowing that she'd hear me wherever she was, I spoke out loud.

'You can visit me any time you want to!'

I sat down on the porch where the little girl had been standing. Hmm, I'd thought about her often. Was she showing herself to me for any particular reason, or was she just passing through? And was how she looked the way she was when she was alive? By that I mean when a spirit showed themselves to me, it's most often in the image or age they actually were when they passed. But when disease had ravaged a person's body, or they had Dementia or Alzheimer's, and had became a shell of their former selves, that person's spirit would show itself as he or she had looked before becoming sick.

So while there was every chance that the little girl in the pink dress was just that, a little girl aged around ten-years-old, there was also a chance that she wasn't. I had to consider that how she was showing herself to me *wasn't* how she looked when she passed, but instead the way which she wished to be remembered, or seen.

Whatever the answer to her identity, only time would tell. But one thing I knew for sure! I sensed strongly that she *wasn't* related to me, and that she *wasn't* anyone that I personally knew.

I was walking through a forest of tall pine trees. It was a warm and sunny day, but the daylight was filtered where I was below a thick canopy of branches. I heard the little girl giggling and turned around to see her run from behind one of the trees and hide behind another tree. She was playing hide and seek. Still giggling, she ran out from behind that tree, and cut across in front of me to hide behind another one.

Then behind me I heard the rustling of footsteps; someone was running towards me through the undergrowth. I turned to see a young man aged around eighteen. His chiselled jaw and looks reminded me of actor, Matt Damon, but rather than give the young man in spirit the obvious name of Matt, I felt compelled to call him Lochie.

Lochie didn't pay me any attention as he ran past me in his search for the little girl. He didn't have to look very hard though because she gave herself away by giggling, and then came out from her hiding place behind a tree and starting running. The young man gave chase. There was nothing sinister about what I was seeing. They were having plain, old fashioned, simple fun.

After that dream with the little girl and Lochie, people from the other side began stepping forward in increasing numbers. While spirits had stepped forward to me in the past, it had always only been one or two spirits at a time. Now there were at least twelve spirits wanting my attention. It was almost as if the little girl's presence had opened a door through which other a larger number of spirits could walk through and make contact with me.

As my first day of filming *Sensing Murder* approached, the number of spirits wanting my attention doubled to about twenty. Whichever spirit wanted the most attention stepped forward the furthest. Unfortunately for me none of the spirits were very vocal. They were just … there, either staring at me in my dreams, or imprinting their faces in my mind when I was awake. How I wished that talking to them was as simple as it's portrayed on TV shows like *The Ghost Whisperer* and *Medium*. Especially on *The Ghost Whisperer*, spirits would often have an in depth conversations with Jennifer Love-Hewitt's character and explain what messages they wanted to pass on, or situation they wanted to resolve. In real life, finding out what spirits want to say isn't that easy.

One of the spirits stepping forward to me was an older man in his late sixties or early seventies. He really wanted to be noticed, and after a couple of days of trying to figure out who he was, I interpreted a couple of spiritual clues which I felt held the answer!

I was still to meet Lisa, but we'd spoken so many times on the phone I felt like I'd known her for years.

'Hi Scott, how are you?'

'Lisa, I'm fine, but there's been some weird shit going on!'

'What kind of weird shit?'

'Well, this is going to sound strange, but I had an elderly man visit me in a dream the other night. I thought at first that he might be connected to one of the *Sensing Murder* cases, but I can't help thinking that this man is the father of someone who's working behind the scenes on the show. Has someone's father just died?'

'Scott, the Executive Producers father died on Friday. She's at his funeral as we speak!'

There was a short pause as Lisa and I took in the moment.

'Was his name Ronald?' I asked.

'I don't know his name,' Lisa told me, 'but I'll check it out and let you know.'

Which Lisa did. The father's name was Ronald!

'Why would he be showing himself to you?' Lisa asked me during our next phone conversation.

'Well, maybe Ronald thought I was the obvious choice since I'm working on his daughter's show,' I said. 'I can always pass on a message to her.'

'She had a feeling he might show himself to you,' Lisa said. 'She told me that the other day. Is there a message by the way?'

'Not that he's telling me. Perhaps he just wanted her to know that he's okay. But if he does pass any message along, I'll let you know.'

On the first two occasions when Ronald visited me he stepped out from the growing group of spirits on his own. By the third occasion he brought a young woman forward with him. I was immediately struck by how beautiful she was. Of Italian or Greek heritage and aged in her early twenties, she had long, wavy, dark hair. I tried to pick up on what her name was. I knew it started with an M, and at first I thought it was something a little out of the ordinary like Mercyndol. But until I knew better I settled on calling her Mercedes.

There were also two other young women standing just behind Ronald. One was definitely called Sarah. I had no doubt that's what her name was because it came across to me loud and clear. If only it was that easy all the time! The other spirit's name was either Cathy or Carol. Were these female spirits part of the *Sensing Murder* cases, or like Ronald, were they showing themselves to me for other reasons?

Only time would tell!

Chapter 4

SENSING MURDER

'Where do you want to take me?' I asked.

'A place,' the little girl in the pink dress whispered in a hushed tone of secrecy.

'A place?' I questioned. She nodded, but I was none the wiser. A place could be anything or anywhere. But knowing how kids like to play guessing games, I didn't push the point. 'Okay, 'I said, 'a place it is!'

The little girl smiled and stepped forward so that I could see her better in the night time darkness. Moonlight caressed her straight fair hair as she reached her hand out to me.

'You want to go there now?' I asked.

She nodded again, so I gently took hold of the little girl's hand and we rose upwards towards the twinkling stars and moon. Then across the countryside we flew, and as we crested a tree-lined hill, the lights of a country town appeared to my left, and the lights of a city were further on in the distance to my right. Flying like Peter Pan and Wendy, the little girl and I crossed the sky and then slowly descended. We landed gently on a dirt road that passed in front of an old style house. No lights were on inside the house, and I shivered because it gave me the creeps! The little girl looked up to me with sombre eyes.

'The bad people are here!' she told me sadly, clutching my hand a little tighter.

When the little girl said "the bad people", I wanted to pick her up and hold her tight and tell her that she was safe with me; that I wouldn't let anything happen to her! But I couldn't do that because I suddenly became frozen, unable to move or speak. The little girl let go of my hand and slowly walked towards the creepy house. Every part of my being wanted to stop her, to yell out: 'Don't go'! But I was frozen and I lost sight of her as she disappeared into the darkness around the house.

Then someone tugged at my left hand! The unexpected movement unfroze my body. I looked to see who it was, expecting to see the little girl. But it wasn't her. It was a young teenage boy!

I sat bolt upright in bed! My dream had been so vivid! I glanced at the glowing red numerals of the bedside clock in my hotel room. It was 4.00 am, and I'd flown into Melbourne the previous evening, was told I'd be staying in Melbourne and not flying on to another location, and was due to start filming in five hours time. I reached for a glass of water that was on the bedside table next to the clock and drank what was left to relieve my parched mouth. I returned the empty glass, settled back into my pillows, and sighed. I'd recognised the boy's face immediately from all the press clippings, magazine articles and television coverage. The boy in my dream was missing Queensland teenager, Daniel Morcombe! I wondered if we'd be doing Daniel's case.

As for the little girl, I still didn't know who she was, and I hadn't given her a temporary name like Sally. To me she was just 'the little girl'. Those three words had become not only her name, but her spiritual identity!

I glanced at the bedside clock for another reminder of how there were only a few hours until filming started. I rolled over and did my best to get some sleep.

At 5.00 am I was standing at the window of my hotel room watching the occasional person wander along the street below. I'd just have to get through my first day of filming as best I could.

It was 9.00 am when Lisa knocked on my hotel door.

'Finally we meet!' she enthused, and we hugged in the doorway. In her early thirties, Lisa had curly shoulder length hair and wore glasses. 'How did you sleep?' she asked.

'I didn't.'

'Are you feeling okay?' she asked.

'Surprisingly, I feel quite good. Is the film crew waiting down in the foyer?'

'No. They're on the sixth floor,' Lisa told me. 'Before we go out on the road we need to get you on camera talking about what you do and how you do it.'

The sixth floor was a private conference room and entertainment area. Lisa and I walked in amongst a mass of lights, cables and a camera. It was here that she introduced me to a number of people, including the cameraman (cammo) and the sound guy (soundie). As hellos were said and I shook hands, I wondered what all those gathered thought of the *Sensing Murder* subject matter. Like most crews I'd worked with over the years, they probably weren't too fazed. They were usually too busy being immersed in whatever their function was on the production. I was then introduced to James the Director. In his late twenties, James had a beaming smile and told me when we finished filming here at the hotel, that we'd go out on the road.

With make up in place, my hair combed neatly, and my shirt quickly ironed, James sat me in front of the camera for the first time and we started filming.

'Scott, when did you first know you were psychic?' Lisa asked.

'When I was seven-years-old I fell backwards off a pier, hit my head against the bow of a boat, and drowned. My dad pulled me out of the water and brought me back. After that l I started seeing ghosts and images of world disasters.'

'That must have been tough to handle as kid,' Lisa said. 'Did you tell anyone what you were going through?'

I shook my head. 'I didn't know what I was going through so I didn't know how to explain it to anyone! I was also scared that people would make fun of me, so I didn't say anything.'

'You mentioned ghosts standing around your bed. How do ghosts appear to you? What do they look like?'

'They look like regular people but they're surrounded by a blue light. How long they stay depends on the energy of the spirit. Those with stronger energies can stay for longer.'

'Do they talk to you like regular people?'

'They can, but more often they communicate with broken sentences or just one word. They can also speak in a foreign language but I'll still understand what they're saying.' I smiled. 'How I do that I have no idea. It just happens that way.

People in spirit can also show me symbols, shapes, colours, or objects, and I have to try to work out what it all means.'

'So mostly you don't hear people in spirit clearly?'

'No, unfortunately. It's mostly like trying to hear someone on a mobile phone and the signal breaks up.'

'Scott, how did your much publicised prediction that Princess Diana was in danger come to you?'

'I dreamt about the cover of a *Woman's Day* magazine, and she wasn't on it. This was back in the days when Diana was on the cover almost every week. The cover had Paris and the Eiffel Tower, but no Diana, and in my dream I asked, 'Why isn't Princess Diana here'? When I woke from the dream I told myself, 'well she must be dead'! As I received more spiritual clues in the months after that dream, it all became clearer and I made the prediction about her.'

'You spoke to Princess Diana how many times?' Lisa asked.

'Nine.'

'Did you warn her not to go to Paris?'

'Yes. On two or three occasions.'

'But she still went.'

'Yes.'

'Why?'

'Because we all have free will … and no matter who advises us, life is full of choices.'

'In 1996 you predicted the September 11 attacks down to the month. Did that also come to you in a dream?'

'Yes. I saw the buildings on fire, people rushing in the streets, and a lot of devastation. I thought a missile had struck the World Trade Centre. I never thought for a moment that commercial planes had flown into the buildings.'

'Scott, could anyone do what you do?' Lisa asked.

'Specifically what I do? I don't know. But I do believe that we're all talented in our own way. Some people are great artists; some play the piano beautifully or excel at sport. I've found success being a psychic.'

Lisa leant forwards in her chair. 'Scott there's something I'd like to show you.'

Lisa handed me an old violin case with a couple of stickers randomly stuck on it like kids at school stick on their book covers and folders.

'Do you pick up anything from this?' Lisa asked.

I held the violin case for a few moments, turned it over, looked at both sides, and then handed it back to Lisa. 'No,' I answered. 'But tell me something. Does the name Mercedes mean anything to anyone here?'

From the startled looks that shot around the room, obviously the name *did* mean something!

'What are you picking up on?' Lisa asked.

'A spirit I'm calling Mercedes, but I know that's not her real name. It's an unusual, European pronunciation. I'll figure out what it is eventually.'

'What does she want?' Lisa asked.

'She wants to take me somewhere, I don't know where. But I feel that if we start driving that she'll lead the way.'

More hushed glances went around the room. Lisa, James and some other members of the *Sensing Murder* crew moved to one side of the room and had a whispered conversation. A minute or so later, Lisa broke away from the others and walked over to me.

'Can you describe Mercedes?' Lisa asked.

'About five foot five, slim, wavy dark hair to just past her shoulders.'

'Age?'

'Twenty to twenty-five.'

Lisa handed me a small white card with a date of birth printed on it. 'Scott as your preferred method of tuning into spirits is through their date of birth, can you tell me if this date belongs to Mercedes?'

If it did I'd usually feel a warm energy in my chest, arms and hands. On this occasion I felt nothing. If anything, my hands were cold.

'I don't think so Lisa,' I said. 'I can't match the energy of this date to her energy.'

Suddenly a jolt of spiritual energy hit me, which startled everyone because I physically jolted in my chair.

'What is it?' asked a startled Lisa.

'When I was a DJ in country radio, one of my favourite duo's was *Loggins & Messina*, the Loggins part of the duo being Kenny Loggins who went on to sing *Footloose*. Why am I thinking of *Loggins & Messina*?' You could have heard a pin drop as the room fell eerily silent. 'The real name of Mercedes wouldn't happen to be "Messina" by any chance?' I asked.

As a flurry of phone calls and activity went on around me, I had some quiet time to take in the surrounds. Right under my feet was a large rug. The rug had an interesting mixture of shapes around its edges, and it was then I noticed something!

'Lisa!' I called out; interrupting the conversation she was having with James.

They both walked over to me and I pointed to the rug. 'That's what Mercedes wants to show me,' I said returning to the name I'd originally called the girl. Until someone confirmed or denied "Messina", I'd stick with "Mercedes".

James and Lisa looked to where I was pointing on the rug.

'See that pattern that looks like bricks in a wall?' I said. 'Above that is a cross. Mercedes wants me to find a cross!' I could almost feel the hair bristle on the back of Lisa's neck. She looked to James.

'First of all,' James said, 'you should know that everyone's a little freaked out right now. What's happened is you were actually flown over to work on Case One, but what you've done is jumped to Case Three. So what we've decided to do is this. One of the other psychics is also in town to work on Case One. All the hurried phone calls you saw happening were to organise a second film crew at short notice so that we can film Case One with her and keep this crew to film Case Three with you, which is the Mercedes Case.' James peered at me intently. 'Did I explain that okay?' he asked.

I nodded. 'Yep.'

'Good. For now I just want you to concentrate on Mercedes. We'll go back to the other case another day.' James looked at his watch. 'You've got half an hour to grab a coffee or freshen up before we leave!'

Chapter 5

FAWKNER CEMETERY

At my request an hour later I was standing in front of the Melbourne GPO. I thought it would be a good central starting point because I didn't know what direction Mercedes wanted me to go in. Also as I was in an unfamiliar city, it was easy for me to lose my sense of direction.

I took a deep breath and blocked out the noise and rush of Melbourne. I was about to learn another lesson in receiving messages from the other side: don't try too hard to interpret what's being passed on. Just say it!

'You guys are going to think this is nuts,' I said, 'but this is what I need to do.'

And with that I did a couple of 360-degree turns in front of the GPO. I was trying to be a spiritual compass and pick up on the direction in which Mercedes energy was coming from the strongest. I pointed and asked, 'which way is that?'

'North,' said Lisa.

'We need to go north then,' I said. 'And there's something to do with Sydney.' I then felt stupid. 'Of course there's something to do with Sydney!' I reasoned out loud. 'Sydney is north of Melbourne!' I looked to Lisa and James. 'Let's head towards Sydney!'

A few minutes later we were on our way, heading north through the Melbourne traffic. I was sitting in the back right-hand corner of the van, peering out the window looking for any symbol or sign that I could connect to the spiritual energy that was coming from Mercedes. Aside from her, the other two female spirits who I'd noticed before had begun to step forward more strongly, and as we journeyed north I felt the need to say their names.

'There are two girls with Mercedes,' I said as the camera filmed every moment. 'One of them is called Sarah. The other is Cathy or Carol.' I paused as a sudden burst of spiritual energy brought another couple of people forward. 'Okay,' now there's another two. There's a little Chinese girl aged about twelve, and a young man who I've seen before. He looks like Matt Damon and has a very chiselled jaw, striking eyes, and is aged about twenty. I feel that he's from the north of Melbourne. Is he also one of your cases?'

As would become the norm, my questions would either be answered with silence, or a question.

'Do you have a name for this young man?' Lisa asked.

'I get the name Lochie, I think it's a nickname. We're definitely heading in the right direction because Mercedes energy is getting stronger all the time!'

'So if we were heading in the wrong direction Mercedes energy would get weaker?' Lisa asked.

'That's right,' I nodded.

'Scott, ask what the name of this road is on camera will you?' James prompted.

'What road is this?' I dutifully asked.

'Sydney Road,' answered Lisa. 'That's why you were picking up on Sydney back at the GPO. We just couldn't tell you at the time.'

'And look!' I said excitedly as I peered out the window. 'Look at the wooden poles that are holding up the electricity wires along this road. They look like a row of large crosses. Like what I saw on the rug back at the hotel, there's the cross symbol again!'

'Get a shot of the poles will you,' James told the cammo.

Another couple of minutes along the road and the energy flowing from Mercedes grew even stronger as the road widened.

'What Mercedes wants me to find is around here somewhere!' I said. There was an air of anticipation in the van. Everyone was perched on the edge of their seats waiting to see what was going to transpire. I peered out the right hand side of the van.

'I'm looking for a cemetery or a church. I'm also looking for a shop; you know one of those old delis with a Coca Cola sign across the bottom of its windows. The shop may not have the Coke sign on it now, but it used to.'

'How many shops?' Lisa asked.

'Three or four together. Just a small group.' Mercedes energy was so strong now I could hardly contain myself. 'The cross is here!' I said with my gaze fixed to the right hand side of the van. 'It's down one of these side streets!' We went a little further. 'Turn right here. This street! This street!'

Like something out of a bad car chase movie we suddenly cut across a couple of lanes of oncoming traffic and into the side street that I was spiritually drawn to. The van slowed down and we cruised along the partly commercial, mainly residential street.

Something caught my eye. 'What's that up ahead?' A small block of shops came into view. 'There! Those shops! That's what I'm looking for!'

We parked outside the shops and got out to stretch our legs.

I pointed to a takeaway shop. 'Someone who has information regarding the case frequented this shop!'

James and the crew moved away from me to film exteriors of the shop and street, and I took a welcome drink from a bottle of spring water.

'How far away from the city are we?' I asked Lisa.

'Around 12 kilometres. What are you picking up on?'

'That I need to walk back down this street towards the main road.'

I didn't ask if that was okay or not. I just walked across the road and headed back towards the main road, retracing the way we came. I didn't know what I was looking for. I just knew the direction I had to walk in. I looked at the houses and street signs to see if Mercedes energy wanted me to go down a side street. But it didn't. It wanted me to go straight ahead!

I heard a vehicle approaching from behind me and looked over my shoulder to see that the van and crew were following me, filming my every move. I crossed a side street and a young woman walked out in front of me. I turned to the van and gestured. She looked exactly like Mercedes! It was almost like she was leading the way!

With only a few houses to walk past before I reached the main road, the girl walked across the street and turned into the main road, disappearing from view. On the corner of the road was a site that sold trucks and commercial vehicles. As I approached the corner, and with the trucks blocking my view, something made me look up and beyond the tops of the trucks … and there it was! Over the other side of the main road was a huge white cross!

Fawkner Cemetery

I became quite emotional at this point. Finding the shop had been one thing, but to find this huge cross! The van parked and Lisa walked over to me as James and the crew scurried across the main road to get the shots they needed.

'It's called the Fawkner Cemetery,' Lisa told me as we both surveyed the cross and surrounds. 'It's one of the biggest cemeteries in Australia!'

'That cross is huge!' I said. It looks about four-storey's tall!'

Lisa smiled. 'When you were in the van saying, it's here, it has to be here, it was just amazing! You were looking out the right-hand side of the van, and the Fawkner Cemetery was on the left. We knew this was what you were looking for, but we couldn't say anything.'

'Did you see that girl walking along the road?' I asked.

'We sure did!' said Lisa. 'That was very spooky!'

Lisa and I stood quietly for a few moments and watched the crew filming.'Is Mercedes' energy still strong?' Lisa asked.

'Very.'

'Well,' she said, 'It's time to tell you a few things.'

Mercedes' real name was Mersina Halvagis. She was twenty-five years old in November 1997 when she visited the Fawkner Cemetery to place flowers on her grandmother's grave late one sunny Saturday afternoon. Mersina was at the gravesite about to put water into matching stone urns, when she was stabbed to death in a vicious, frenzied attack.

Mersina Halvagis

Mersina came from a hard-working Greek family and was a very friendly and compassionate person. As far as her family knew, she didn't have any enemies. At first it was believed that the murderer could have a psychiatric illness or be a thrill killer who lurked in the cemetery waiting for a victim

We drove into Fawkner Cemetery through its northern gates, and stopped at one of the first parking areas we came to. From outside, Fawkner Cemetery looked huge, but only now once inside did I get a true indication of just how big this place was! It must have been the size of three or four suburbs!

'Any chance of finding the grandmother's grave?' Lisa asked me.

I looked across a sea of different headstones, statues, and crosses. 'I'm picking up on so many people from the other side here I don't like my chances of doing that,' I answered.

I'd promised myself that I'd be honest all the time. If I didn't know something, I'd say so. Lisa led the way and we walked along gravel paths to where the final resting place of Mersina's grandmother was. The inscription on the grave was written in Greek, so I couldn't read it.

'Listen,' I said. 'I need time out for a sec. Can I walk around on my own, see what I pick up?'

Lisa nodded. 'Sure.'

So I wandered over to a nearby creek that was lined with trees. It looked quite scenic from a distance, but on closer inspection the creek was dry and littered with drink cans and rubbish. I didn't get much of a feeling from around the creek, and wasn't drawn to investigate any other direction, so I wandered back to the others to reveal a summary of my thoughts.

'The shops I found were important because I believe either the person who attacked Mersina, or someone who witnessed the attack on her frequented those shops. I'm picking up on a man who's in his early thirties, tall with short-cropped curly hair. His skin is either tanned or he could be part Aboriginal. There is also the name Doug, Dougie or Douglas. This could be a first or a last name. I feel he witnessed what happened and ran away when he startled the attacker. He ran out through the northern gates that we drove through just over there. I believe that Doug was in the cemetery with the intent of committing some kind of sexual assault, but not murder. I also feel a connection between Doug a psychological assessment facility within a two to five kilometre radius of here. Perhaps he had counselling there.

A couple of people visiting graves here on the day Mersina was killed heard what happened, and a person working here at the cemetery saw or came into contact with the perpetrator on the day. I'm not sure if that person still works here. Mersina's attacker is a man with medium to dark hair, aged in his late thirties or early forties at the time. I'm feeling the name Paul, but the energy around that name isn't overly strong, so it may not be related to this case.' I looked around the cemetery. 'Paul could even be someone who's buried here. I'm not sure.'

'What about the name Peter?' Lisa said. 'In any way can you associate the name Peter with Mersina?'

I focused on the name Peter for a moment. 'There is some energy around that name,' I answered, 'but the strongest name I have now is Paul, not Peter.'

Unbeknownst to me I was starting to segue way into the next case I'd film, because the name Paul would feature then.

'Do you feel the perpetrator is free, or in jail?' Lisa asked.

'The strongest feeling I have is that he's already in jail.'

Lochie then unexpectedly appeared in front of one of the graves. He smiled as he looked to me, casually observing what we were doing. His presence distracted me.

'Guys, you have to go through your records and see if you can find a young man around twenty years of age who looks like Matt Damon. The spirit I'm seeing has a chiselled jaw and piercing eyes. He's not anything to do with the Mersina Case, but he keeps showing himself to me because he wants to be recognised. His name is either Lochie or maybe Lachlan. Can anyone think of what else Lochie might be short for?' No one could. 'Stick with Lachlan then,' I said. 'I think he's from the north of Melbourne, maybe even country Victoria ... somewhere like Mildura up near the border.'

'I'll check it out,' said Lisa as she made a note on her clipboard.

'So Lisa,' I sighed, grateful that the pressure of filming was over. 'What happens now with the information I've given you?'

'It'll all be passed on to private investigators. They'll check out all the scenarios and people you've mentioned and hopefully confirm and validate your psychic clues.'

'So if a worker in the cemetery did see the perpetrator,' I said, 'the private investigators will try and find them?'

'Yep.'

A worker at the Fawkner Cemetery told police that she'd spoken to a man resembling serial killer Peter Dupas on the day of the murder. The worker was looking after the

Latvian section of Fawkner Cemetery when a man approached her about 9.30 am. The man said his name was John Roberts, and that he had just found the grave of his adoptive mother, whom he had never met. The worker gave the man a rake to tidy the grave.

In April 1998 the worker provided police with a computer-generated drawing of the man. In August 2000 the worker saw a photo of Dupas on the front page of a newspaper and realised it was the man she'd spoken to at the cemetery.

During a 2005 inquest into the Mersina Halvagis Case several witnesses said they saw a man resembling Dupas at the cemetery on the day Mersina was murdered. Police had considered Dupas a prime suspect since 1999. Amongst clues considered were that Dupas frequented a pub nearby to the Fawkner Cemetery, and that

the graves of Mersina's grandmother and Dupas's grandfather were
less than 100 metres apart.

With a week off after filming the Mersina Case I tried to relax as best I could, but that turned out to be wishful thinking, because there were now more than thirty spirits vying for my attention, sending me thoughts, symbols and images – all at the same time!

Lisa phoned during that week and told me there was a problem with the Mersina Case. Mersina's father George had relentlessly pursued every paper, TV, radio and magazine to keep his daughter's memory alive, and hopefully spark the memory of a member of the public who may have seen something. But some of the Halvagis family members weren't so keen to be in the spotlight, so George withdrew their participation in *Sensing Murder*. When Mersina's family withdrew, so did Mersina's friends, and without the involvement of those key loved ones, the Mersina Case was dropped from the *Sensing Murder* line-up, and the process then began to find a replacement Case because Channel Ten had commissioned six movie-length episodes.

I'd even surprised myself with how I was able to lead the crew when filming the Mersina case. I was on such a personal high during the days after filming, that I quickly pushed aside my memories of the lack of sleep that accompanied the process. But when the Mersina Case was dropped, I came crashing back to earth very quickly, and all the difficulties of the psychic process involved pushed their way to the front of my thinking again. While I understood and empathised with why the case was dropped, from where I was standing I felt that I'd gone to a whole lot of trouble for nothing. And what if it happened again? What if another case got dropped?! Was it really worth me to go through all the trouble and effort I did if at the end of the day it was for nothing?

2015 Update

The Victorian State Government offered a one million dollar reward for information leading to an arrest in the Mersina Halvagis case. An elderly man, Frank Cole would later claim that he saw known sex offender Peter Dupas leaving the Fawkner Cemetery on the day of Mersina's murder. A woman who was visiting her parents' grave on the same day also claimed to have seen Dupas.

An inquest into Mersina's death heard circumstantial evidence against Peter Dupas in relation to the murder.

Nine witnesses identified Dupas as a man they saw at Fawkner Cemetery on the day Halvagis was attacked.

Dupas' grandfather's gravesite is located 128 metres from the crime scene.

Dupas frequented the 'First and Last Hotel', located opposite Fawkner Cemetery.

Dupas lied to police about a facial injury received about the time of the attack on Halvagis.

Dupas attempted to alter his appearance after Halvagis' murder.

Dupas was identified by a woman from police photographs, who said she saw him minutes before the attack twenty metres from where Halvagis' murder occurred.

Police told the inquest that a car known to be used by Dupas at the time of the murder was sold to a work associate in the month following the murder. The car had since been crushed for scrap metal and was never examined by detectives.

On September 11, 2006, police charged Dupas with the murder of Mersina Halvagis after a disgraced Melbourne lawyer revealed that Dupas had confessed to her killing while in Port Phillip Prison during 2002.

The Supreme Court of Victoria ordered Dupas be presented directly to trial for the murder, bypassing the usual committal hearing process. Dupas was found guilty on August 9, 2007 and was sentenced to his third life sentence with no minimum term. A month later lawyers for Dupas lodged an appeal.

On September 17, 2009, Dupas's appeal against the conviction was upheld in Victoria's Court of Appeal by a two to one majority. The Court ruled that the directions of the judge in the original trial were inadequate. Lawyers for Dupas argued that the proceedings against him should be stayed permanently based on the publicity surrounding the case. But Victorian Supreme Court Justice Paul Coghlan disagreed, and on October 26, 2010, a new trial for the murder of Mersina Halvagis commenced.

On November 19, 2010, Peter Dupas was again convicted of Mersina's murder after three and half days of deliberations by the jury. He was sentenced to life in prison without the possibility of parole.

Chapter 6

THE BEAUMONT CHILDREN

A private investigator called Lee had been working with me for five years in trying to solve the mystery of the missing Beaumont children. Just like me, Lee had grown up in the Glenelg area only a few streets away from where the Beaumont children lived, so he had his own sentimental reasons for wanting to bring the case to some kind of closure. Lee was like a dog with a bone. He just wouldn't let go of any lead he was pursuing, and would dig and dig until he found a definite outcome one way or the other. In his late forties, Lee and I had known each other for over ten years. He was amongst the most intuitive and level-headed people I knew. He always had a smile, and his nature was … well, the only way I can describe it is constant. He always worked through anything methodically and evenly. And although immersed in reality, fact and commonsense, Lee didn't consider himself a sceptic. He believed that some people *did* have a spiritual gift, and he was totally open to what our combined efforts might achieve on the Beaumont Case. Lee and I would catch up regularly at a café to discuss progress with his investigations.

'Glad to have a week off from *Sensing Murder*?' Lee asked.

I nodded. 'You bet.'

'You look a little worse for wear,' he added, peering at me over the rim of his coffee cup.

I smiled. 'I'm okay.'

'Still got people talking in your head twenty-four-seven?' Lee asked.

'Yep.'

'How are you coping with that?'

'Well … I just am. I mean there's no hard and fast rulebook on how to talk to dead people. I'm just learning as I go.'

'So Scott, even right at this minute they're talking to you?'

'Uh huh, chatting away in the background.'

'So how do you block out what they're saying so that you and I can talk?'

'Well, I kind of just push what they're saying to one side,' I said, 'I little like when you've got the TV or radio on in the background but you can still concentrate on what you're doing.'

'Hmm,' Lee pondered. 'Doesn't it drive you mad when you go to bed? Must be like trying to go to sleep when the neighbours are having a party!'

'That's a good analogy,' I said. 'It's often like that! But, enough of all that. What did you want to tell me?'

Over the years, the eldest of the Beaumont children, Jane, had been passing on spiritual clues to me from the other side. Amongst various symbols and sentences was a name – Alfred.

'I found him!' Lee told me excitedly as we sat at a table in the crowded café. 'I found Alfred!'

'Did he live at Glenelg at the time the Beaumont children disappeared?' I asked.

'Yes,' Lee confirmed. 'And from what I've been told he was quite an unsavoury character! You're talking about a man who used to raffle off his wife to his mates at Saturday night card nights so that they could have sex with her. He also physically and sexually abused his children, both male and female.'

'Does he still live in the Glenelg area?' I asked.

'No he moved on years ago.'

'Do you know where to?'

'Yes.'

'Is he still alive?'

'As far as I know.'

'And his family?'

'They live in the country as far away from him as possible. They're basically in hiding. I had to move slowly and carefully to get any information out of them, and even then, they were reluctant to speak.' Lee leant forward and rested his arms on the table. 'One of his daughters told me that he looks very much like the man in the identikit picture released at the time the Beaumont children disappeared. She also told me that one of the kids got up the guts to call the police and report their father, but nothing happened.'

'Can we link Alfred to our spiritual anchor?' I asked.

'I'm still checking that out,' Lee said.

Spiritual anchor is the term I give to what I believe is the main clue of a case, around which all other aspects of the spiritual investigation must fit. In the Mersina Case, the spiritual anchor had been the cross at Fawkner cemetery. In the Beaumont Case the spiritual anchor was my belief that the children were taken by someone the eldest girl, Jane, knew and trusted.

A little boy aged about five-years-old ran past our table at the café. He was laughing and enjoying himself about nothing in particular has kids are meant to do. Grant Beaumont used to do the same thing; he was such a tearaway as a kid, always getting into everything.

'Do you want another coffee Scott?' Lee asked.

'Thanks.'

'I'll be right back.'

Lee got up from the table and joined a group of people who were waiting at the counter to place their orders. My mind was awash with Beaumont memories. As a kid, I spent a lot of time with Jane, Arnna and Grant. We enjoyed an idyllic childhood, roaming the sandhills, scrub, vineyards and vacant land that was abundant around Glenelg in those days. It was a close-knit, caring community with lots of barbeques and card nights. When I played with the Beaumont children at their house, there was always laughter, music, and a sandwich or a sausage roll. Jim and Nancy were wonderful, caring parents who gave everything to their children, and welcomed all the other neighbourhood kids into their home with open arms.

Even as a little kid my psychic talents were working overtime. I'd warned Jane's best friend Tracy not to go to the beach with the Beaumont children on the day they disappeared. 'You just don't want me to go because you want me to come around to your place instead!' Tracy told me. But it wasn't that. I just had a feeling that something wasn't right. As it turned out, Tracy didn't end up going to the beach that day because her parents had just bought her a new wading pool for Christmas, and couldn't see the sense in having bought the pool if she was still going to favour the beach. If Tracy *had* gone to the beach that Australia Day, would she and the Beaumont children have been taken, or would there have been safety in numbers? I'd thought about the what ifs often, but quickly learnt that travelling down "what if" road is one of the most useless and unproductive things you do. You just have to get on with life and deal with what *did* happen!

When Lee returned to the table with our second round of coffees, I told him about a strange man who had been at a barbeque a couple of months before the Beaumont children disappeared.

The smell of sizzling sausages filled the air. There was a joyous buzz in the air of family, friends and neighbours sharing stories and laughing, happy that the weekend had arrived. Kids ran around the backyard happily yelling to each other, and I watched as a little boy ran face first into old Mrs Johnson's bum as she talked to some elderly women. Mrs Johnson was startled by the sudden invasion to her rear, and the little boy started crying. His Mum came to his rescue and Mrs Johnson attempted to remain dignified and lady-like.

I knew most of the familiar faces here today. They were the usual crowd from around the neighbourhood, except for a couple of people I didn't know including a man who was talking to the Beaumont children's father, Jim Beaumont. The man was in his late twenties or early thirties. He was tall, suntanned and fair, and he didn't have a beer gut like a lot of the other blokes at the barbeque did. He laughed as something funny was said, but there was
something about this man that I didn't like! I had that uneasy feeling you get when you're walking down a dark street and you hope that no one will jump out from the shadows and grab you.

I stifled a yawn; l was getting bored, so I decided to find my friend Jane. I got up from the fold-up chair I was sitting on and navigated my way through the crowd, around the side of the house and down the driveway. A small brick wall bordered the property, so I stepped up onto it and surveyed both ways up and down the footpath and the tree-lined street. There was a row of cars parked either side of the street, and I assumed most of them belonged to the people at the barbie. Seeing nothing of interest I jumped down from the wall and walked across the lawn towards the house. That's when I saw Jane sitting on the front porch.

'There you are!' I said. I sat down next to her and wrapped my arms around my legs. 'I'm bored,' I announced as I rested my chin on my knees.

'Me too,' Jane said.

We sat silently for a few moments, noise and laughter from the barbecue filtering around us.

'Want to go for a walk?' I asked.

'Where?'

'Dunno. Round the block, down to the beach?'

'No,' she said, after considering the possibility. 'Mum and Dad'll worry if they can't find us.'

'Well tell 'em where we're goin',' I suggested.

Jane pondered my suggestion. 'Nah,' she finally replied, and went on to tell me how her younger brother and sister were having a sleep, and that she'd promised her parents that she'd keep an eye on them.

'How old was Jane then?' Lee asked.

'She'd just turned nine.'

'How old were you?'

'Seven.'

'How would you could describe Jane as a person?'

'Well,' I said, 'she was caring, thoughtful, and always wanted to do the right thing by her mum and dad. She was a mother hen, and wouldn't let anyone near her brother and sister. As a matter of fact she was protective of *all* of us kids! She was the eldest of the group, and she never left us younger ones out of her sight. I always felt very safe around her. There was one day at the beach when me and Jane's best friend Tracy were with the Beaumont children, and a man came over to us while we were playing in the shallows. Jane herded us all together, and while she was very police to the man, she didn't let him near us.'

'What do you think he wanted?' Lee asked.

'As the adult I am now, I can only assume the worst,' I said. 'But as the kid I was then, I thought he was just a friendly guy who wanted to say hello. He offered to take us all for ice creams. Jane said no.'

'And,' Lee reiterated, 'our spiritual anchor is that Jane would never have let the children go with a stranger.'

'That's right. And I'm not the only person who thinks that either. None of the people I spoke to who were close to the Beaumont family believe a stranger took the children! And Jim Beaumont told detectives the children would never have gone with a stranger. He said that even though Jane was nine, she had the brain of a fifteen-year-old, and that if Jane weren't as switched on that they would never have been allowed go to the beach on their own!' I paused. 'Lee, all us kids went to the beach on our own back in those days. It was the norm. We didn't give it a second thought.'

Jane, Grant and Arrna - The Beaumont Children

On the morning of Australia Day, 26 January 1966, Jane (9), Arnna (7) and Grant (4) hounded their mother Nancy to let them go to the beach. With the temperature set to soar the children wanted to go for a swim at the seaside suburb of Glenelg, a destination they often visited on their own. With their father Jim at work that day it was left up to Nancy to make the decision. The children wanted to ride their bikes to the beach, but because it was going to be such a hot day Nancy said that they had to catch the bus. Nancy gave Jane eight shillings and sixpence for bus fares and lunch, asking Jane to bring her home a pasty. She also told Jane the children were to catch the midday bus home. Nancy kissed the children goodbye at the front gate and watched them walk hand-in-hand towards the bus stop, which was just around the corner on a busy road. Halfway down the street Jane, Arnna and Grant turned back to Nancy and waved. That was the last time Nancy ever saw them.

Lee sipped his coffee and flicked to a new page of his small notebook.

'Who do you reckon the man at the barbeque was, the one who you didn't like?'

'Don't know,' I answered. 'That was the only time I saw him, and I'd forgotten all about him until just recently. Maybe he was Alfred.'

'That would be something wouldn't it,' Lee said as he flicked back to the previous page of his notebook and read what he'd written. 'You described this man as being in his late twenties or early thirties, tall, suntanned and fair. That pretty much describes the man seen playing with the children on the beach the day they disappeared.'

'Yeah, but the man seen with the children was also described as gaunt. The guy I saw at the barbecue wasn't gaunt. He was athletic looking and muscular, and had longer hair.'

'Maybe he lost some weight and got a haircut between the time of the barbeque and when the children disappeared,' Lee suggested. He took a sheet of paper from a folder that was resting on the table. 'Did he look like this?' he asked, showing me one of the most memorable images in Australian media history.

Beaumont Suspect Sketch 1 and Sketch 2

'Yeah he did,' I said, 'although there's something about that sketch you should know. The man who drew it admitted he was a little worse for wear after having a couple of drinks at the pub just before he was asked to draw it. Apparently he didn't get a really good description from witnesses either.'

'Hmm,' said Lee as he studied the image. 'I've seen this sketch with the eyes filled in, and with glasses too I think.'

Beaumont Suspect Sketch 3

'Well,' said Lee thoughtfully. 'Regardless of whether the artist finished the sketch properly or not, between the sketch, the man seen playing with the children at the beach and the man you saw at the barbeque, the main suspect is still a tall, blonde man! Scott, you said the day that after the children disappeared, three or four friends of the Beaumont's helped in the search and saw someone they believed could be the man in the sketch.'

I nodded. 'That's right. And they all described him as tall and lanky, and said that he reminded them of the actor who played the farmer in the movie *Babe*.'

'James Cromwell,' Lee prompted.

'That's him. Anyway, the man who looks like James Cromwell was seen on the beach at Brighton (further down from Glenelg), and he was also seen at a caravan park in that same area.'

'Which caravan park?'

'They can't remember the name, and when I went looking for it when they told where it was, I couldn't find it. I assume they've built houses on the land now, but I can give you directions to where it was located.'

'Good, and I'll check it out,' said Lee. 'Now let's go through the key contenders again, just to see if your psychic feeling on any of these people or scenarios has changed.' Lee flipped back a few pages in his notebook. 'Jim and Nancy Beaumont?'

I shook my head. 'Absolutely not!'

Lee read out the next heading. 'Blood Relative?'

'No.'

'A trusted neighbour or friend who was known as an "Uncle"?'

'I still get the strongest feeling from that possibility,' I said. 'I mean back in those days every neighbour was an uncle or auntie, unlike today where kids tend to call grown-ups by their first names unless they actually are a relative.'

Lee read the next title. 'Priest?'

'Maybe, but the Beaumont's weren't really churchy people.'

'Teacher?'

'Yeah, a possible thought was a teacher from Jane's school. But Jane never mentioned a teacher that she liked or disliked. I don't pick up any spiritual energy around that possibility either, so I'd be inclined to rule it out.'

'Other possibilities?' Lee asked.

'Well,' I said. 'Who made enough money in those days to give Jane a one pound note? And who did she trust enough to take the one-pound note from? A one-pound in 1966 was a hell of a lot of money, and as a kid I can't ever recall seeing a one-pound note. Has anyone ever questioned what kind of job a person would have to hold to be able to flash around such a lot of money! Jane would've known it was a lot of money too, but she obviously felt okay to take it because "Uncle whoever" dealt with that kind of money all the time!'

'Indeed!' Lee nodded. 'Well the person was either wealthy, or ran a business where there was ready cash.'

'He could have been a bookie,' I suggested. 'There were plenty of bookies around Glenelg back then. I remember Nancy liking a bet. Where would she go to put a bet on if she couldn't make it to the pub? There'd have to be a bookie nearby. What if the bookie is our barbeque guy? The other thing is that Jane keeps showing me *one* image in particular: a *horse!* I can't help but think that the image is related to one of the many stables that were operating in and around Glenelg at the time, that the man or men who took the children either worked at, or had connections to a stable.'

'Yes there certainly were a lot of stables around Glenelg then,' agreed Lee, 'but they're gone now. These days there's houses and units built on all that land.' He paused to write something down and to drink his coffee. So,' Lee said thoughtfully. 'I'm looking for a possible paedophile link to one of the stables that was operating in and around Glenelg back when the children disappeared. You're pretty keen on the stable scenario aren't you, Scott? I don't sense any doubt or hesitation when you talk about it.'

'Well,' I said, besides Jane showing me the horse, there's a couple of other reasons for my lack of hesitation. I've told you before about how I was sexually assaulted by three men on Glenelg Beach when I was thirteen years old.' Lee nodded. 'Well one of the men smelt like leather and straw, like he worked at a stable!'

'Did any of the men who attacked you look like the guy in the sketch?' Lee asked.

'I really only got a good look at the ringleader, and he didn't look like the guy in the sketch. I never saw the faces of the other two.'

'You said there were a couple of reasons?' Lee prompted.

I sighed. 'Yeah, there is.' I sat forward and rested my arms on the table. 'When I was fifteen I visited Jim and Nancy, and I saw Grant standing in the corner of their lounge room … he was a ghost. Anyway, he was wearing his bathers and he smiled to me, and I thought it was odd that instead of smelling the beach when I saw him, that I smelt horses and hay!'

Lee made a note. 'And Scott, you say that you keep "seeing" a make of car which you believe was either involved in the children's disappearance, or were connected to the case in some way?'

'Yep, A 1964 pale blue EH Holden with a white roof. They don't paint cars like that anymore, but having that two-tone effect was popular back in the sixties and seventies.'

The colour drained from Lee's face. He slumped back in his chair.

'What's wrong?' I asked.

Lee took a breath, sat forward, and rested his hands on the table.

'In 1970 when I was fifteen, I was coming back from a mate's place one night. It was about 9.00 pm, I'd missed my bus, and it was a school night so my parents didn't want me home too late. Anyway, instead of hanging around waiting for another bus, I decided to hitchhike; everyone hitchhiked back then. A guy offered me a lift to Glenelg, about a ten-minute drive from where I was. A couple of minutes into the ride and he tried to crack on to me, so at the next set of traffic lights I bailed and ran like the wind! He was driving a pale blue 1964 EH Holden with a white roof!'

1964 pale blue EH Holden with a white roof

Lee!' I said. 'You've just turned out to be a bigger part of the Beaumont jigsaw puzzle than just being the private investigator!'

Lee nodded. 'It would appear that way, yes … unless it's just a coincidence.'

'There are no coincidences,' I said.

'Hmm,' Lee pondered, 'the more time I spend with you, the more I see the truth in that.'

'How hard would it be to track the car down?' I asked, 'And preferably narrowing the search down to someone who lived in the Glenelg area in 1966.'

'Near impossible!' Lee said. 'To the best of my knowledge car records that go back that far are no longer in existence.'

'That's disappointing,' I said.

'And with all the strict privacy laws that are in place now,' Lee added, 'I probably wouldn't have been able to get my hands on the records anyway.'

'Then,' I said, 'we need to return our attention to who took the children!

10.10 am

The Beaumont children caught a bus to the beach. The bus driver confirmed the children were on his bus. He knew them because they were regulars. A woman passenger also saw them, and told police what colours the clothes were that the children were wearing, and that Jane had a copy of Little Women, a book she had left the house with.

10.15 am

The bus stopped in Moseley Street in the heart of Glenelg. It's assumed the children got off the bus here and walked the short distance to the beach because several eyewitnesses, including a friend of Jane's from school saw the children walking between the bus stop and the beach. They were then seen playing in the shallows near the Glenelg jetty.

11.00 AM

A 74-year-old woman sitting on a bench in front of the Holdfast Bay Yacht Club saw two girls and a boy walk towards her from the ocean after a swim. They laid out their towels on lawns near two trees, and began playing under a sprinkler. The woman said she didn't notice anyone else with them. What attracted her attention later was a tall, blond-haired surfie looking man who was talking to the children. Aged in his mid-to-late thirties, he'd been sunbaking on a towel nearby and was wearing Speedo-type navy blue bathers. The woman told police that the children had gone over to the man, and that he was laughing and encouraging them as they played. The boy and younger girl were jumping over him, and the older girl was flicking the man with a towel.

11.30 AM

The woman left the beach to walk home and cook dinner. The children and the man were still playing on the lawn.

11.45 AM

The Beaumont children entered Wenzel's Bakery in Moseley Street near the bus stop and bought lunch with a one-pound note. Police believe the person who gave them the one-pound note remained outside the shop while they made their purchases. Nancy Beaumont was adamant that she'd only given Jane six shillings and sixpence. The shopkeeper knew the children and said they bought their usual pasties, plus an extra item, a meat pie. Who was the meat pie for? The children were due to catch the midday bus home in fifteen minutes time.

MIDDAY ONWARDS

Although there were other reported sightings of the children at Glenelg after midday, including one by a local postman who knew them, none of these sightings could be confirmed. Police consider the last official and confirmed sighting of the Beaumont children to be when they bought their lunch at Wenzel's Bakery.

When the children didn't come home on the midday bus like Nancy had told them to, she wasn't overly concerned, figuring that they'd decided to walk home so they could spend their bus fare on lollies. Jim Beaumont arrived home from work later in the afternoon. There was still no sign of the children so he went looking for them. In the early evening he notified police and a massive search was launched. By morning the Beaumont children were front-page news across the nation. At first police believed they'd run away, drowned, or been abducted and were being held for ransom.

'When the children left the beach, what do you believe happened?' Lee asked.

'Well,' I began, 'I don't believe the children were bundled into a car. It was a stinking hot summer's day. The only cars back in those days that had air conditioning were predominantly "yank tanks": big American cars that very few people had. So there's no way that a single person, or even two people got three children to quietly get into a car against their will, especially when that vehicle was a furnace inside after being parked in the summer's sun for a few hours! If they were in a car, the car windows would have been down, and if they were being held against their will or going in the wrong direction, someone would have noticed something because one or more of the children would have made some noise, especially Jane! And as most of the routes out of Glenelg involve traffic lights, if they'd stopped at the lights most likely someone would have seen something then. No,' I said, 'the children were happy to accept a lift from whoever offered it to them. They knew the person, and I don't think they followed a route that involved traffic lights. I think they cut through some back streets instead. I believe the children were driven south down Moseley Street. Jane would have been more than comfortable with that because going that way was a direct route towards their house. I believe it all started innocently enough, with the simple offer of a lift home from somebody they knew. At that stage, there was no intention of harming anybody. But once in the car I can see Grant sitting in the front seat in his bathers, with his little bare chest, and that's when the "Uncle" started to entertain his paedophile temptation. Grant became the main target, and under the pretence of being offered a cool drink on the way home, the children were lured to a nearby location, possibly stables, and that's as far as they got!'

Jim & Nancy Beaumont

With no sign of the children and public emotions running high, Dutch psychic Gerard Croiset was brought to Australia from the Netherlands which caused a media frenzy! Croiset believed the children's bodies had been buried at a site near their home. At the time of their disappearance it had been a building site, and Croiset believed their bodies were buried under new concrete inside the remains of an old brick kiln. The owners of the property were reluctant to excavate the site on the basis of a psychic's claim, however they bowed to public pressure and allowed a thorough search of the area. Nothing was found

Two years after the children disappeared Jim and Nancy Beaumont received two letters - one supposedly written by Jane, and another by a man who said he was keeping the children. The envelopes were postmarked Dandenong, Victoria. The letters described the children as having a relatively pleasant existence and the letter supposedly written by Jane referred to The Man who was keeping them. At the time police believed there was a good chance the letters were authentic after they compared the handwriting to other letters written by Jane. The letter from The Man said that he had appointed himself guardian of the children and was willing to hand them back to their parents. He nominated a meeting place that Jim and Nancy Beaumont drove to (followed by a detective), but nobody appeared. A supposed further letter from Jane soon arrived saying that The Man had been willing to return the children, but when he'd seen that the police were involved he decided to keep the children because Jim and Nancy had broken his trust. There were no further letters. Twenty-five years later advances in forensic examination proved the letters were a hoax. A forty-one-year-old man admitted that he wrote the letters as a joke when he was a teenager. Due to the elapsed time between when he wrote the letters and when he was identified, the man wasn't charged.

1996

The building identified by Gerard Croiset was undergoing partial demolition and the owners allowed for a full search of the site. Once again no trace was found of the children, but it highlighted the level of ongoing commitment in trying to solve the Beaumont Case even thirty years after their disappearance.

1998

Arthur Stanley Brown was named as a suspect. Then eighty-six-years-old, he'd been charged with the murders of seven-year-old Judith MacKay and her five-year-old sister, Susan. The girls lived in Townsville, Queensland and disappeared on their way to school on 26 August 1970. Their bodies were found several days later in a dry creek bed. Both girls had been strangled. Brown bore a similarity to *the suspect in the Beaumont Case but nothing could be proved because Brown had deteriorated too much mentally, was never retried. He died in 2002.*

2004

New Zealand police investigated claims that the Beaumont children might be living in Dunedin after a man told a woman at a butcher shop that he thought he'd lived next door to the missing children. Later, when the woman read a magazine article about the Beaumont Case, she realised the man's claims may have been valid and contacted police. After a police investigation the children in question were found not to be the Beaumont children.

2005

Tasmanian Police Commissioner Richard McCreadie claimed that Tasmanian prisoner James O'Neill could be responsible for kidnapping the Beaumont children. O'Neill is alleged to have confessed to murdering the Beaumont Children and associates of O'Neill had told documentary filmmakers them that O'Neill killed the Beaumont children. But police couldn't find any evidence to support O'Neill's involvement in the disappearance of the Beaumont children.

2005

The television program Today Tonight claimed to have new evidence about the disappearance of the Beaumont children and said it may have uncovered a new suspect. The claims were based on an apparent abduction attempt from Glenelg beach a day or two before the Beaumont children disappeared.

2005

Victoria's longest serving prisoner Derek Percy was interviewed by cold-case detectives about the Beaumont children. Percy was in Adelaide when the Beaumont children disappeared, and it was believed police could place him near the scene. Percy has been in jail since 1969 over a murder at Western Port Beach which he was found unfit to plea on the grounds of insanity. His writings describing ways of abducting, murdering and mutilating children were found in his cell after he was sentenced.

2005

South Australian Police Minister, Kevin Foley, announced that the reward relating to the Beaumont children disappearance had been increased to $100,000. The increase was made at the request of the South Australia Police Commissioner, Mal Hyde. Just 48 hours after the Beaumont children vanished, a reward of £850 was posted. With the introduction of decimal currency on 14 February 1966 (three weeks after the children disappeared), the initial reward was converted to $1,000 and had not been increased since.

'And where are the children now?' Lee asked.

'We'll talk about that another time,' I said. 'For now, check out the caravan park, check out the stables. That's enough to go on with.'

'Indeed!' said Lee closing his notebook. 'I'll be in touch!'

Chapter 7

I PROMISE

As I drove home from the café a dark-coloured 1964 EH Holden drove past me in the opposite direction. Spirit always has a way of giving a sign or synchronicity! What were the chances that on the same night I'd talked about an EH Holden possibly being involved in the Beaumont Case, that I'd also see one? I felt drawn to drive to Glenelg!

Twenty minutes later I was cruising the familiar streets of Glenelg. The biggest difference between the way Glenelg looks now and how it looked when I was a kid is the amount of high-rise. There were maybe two high-rise buildings in Glenelg when I was growing up. Now numerous high-rise buildings dominate the seaside skyline. An open area where I used to play by the beach is now occupied by a massive multi-level car park, apartments and a marina.

I drove my car into the main street of Glenelg which is Jetty Road, and then turned down Moseley Street where I drove slowly past Wenzel's Bakery; still there after all these years and of course it was closed this time of night, Wenzel's being the last official sighting of the Beaumont children was made.

I followed Moseley Street down towards a popular road called The Broadway, a landmark road in the area comprising mostly of residential housing, a handful of small businesses and a couple of pubs. This is the way I felt the children had been driven. I turned left onto The Broadway and then it happened like it always did when I drove along here; I lost the spiritual scent of exactly where the children went to next. I'd even tried my spiritual compass routine here a couple of times - like I had at the Melbourne GPO - turning in full circle to see which direction I felt the children's energy coming from the most. But unlike the success I'd had in Melbourne, it hadn't worked here! Just why, I didn't know. But one thing was for sure. With Lee's help I felt confident that I'd eventually figure out exactly which street the children went down and where they went from there. I was determined to crack the Beaumont Case because Jane, Arnna and Grant deserved to come home at last!

Something distracted me. I peered across The Broadway and saw the little girl in the pink dress standing on the footpath. I turned off my car's engine and walked across the road. Being a Tuesday night just after 9.45 pm, there was an occasional car and pedestrian, but by no means was it busy compared to during the day and on weekends when this area teemed with people.

'Hello,' I said to the little girl as I stepped onto the footpath where she was standing. The blue light shimmered around her body, and it seemed brighter, more intense than I'd seen it before. She giggled and suddenly turned, running along the footpath away from me. I followed her. Up ahead, the little girl stood on a street corner waiting for me, and as she did, a male pedestrian walked straight past without noticing her. Of course he wouldn't see her I reminded myself. She's a ghost!

The little girl faded from sight. I picked up my pace to make it to the street corner where she'd been standing. I looked down the adjoining side street and there she was quite a distance down the street, a spiritual blue beacon in the night.

I quickly made my way along the street to where she was. The little girl took off again just before I reached her and played hide-and-seek with me along a couple of other streets until eventually, she stayed put outside one particular house. When I caught up to her she pointed towards the house.

'The bad people were here,' the little girl told me. She looked up to me, her eyes filled with sadness and innocence. 'The bad people!' she said again. And a shiver ran down my spine, not only because of what she was telling me, but because Grant Beaumont suddenly appeared next to her on the footpath, also surrounded in blue spiritual light. And just as I'd seen him many years before at the Beaumont house, Grant was wearing his bathers. He smiled to me and the little girl held his hand.

'Grant, I'll find out what happened,' I said. 'I promise!'

Grant smiled, and he and the little girl faded from sight.

In the darkness of a Tuesday night in South Glenelg, had the little girl led me to the house where the Beaumont children had been taken to all those years ago in 1966? Did they come from the beach to here? I sighed. There were clues to what happened to the Beaumont children scattered all over Glenelg. I was determined to put those clues together!

Chapter 9

SARAH & NATHAN

Five days after seeing the little girl at Glenelg, I flew back to Melbourne in preparation to film another case for *Sensing Murder*. As a taxi drove me from the airport to my hotel in South Yarra, I thought about the house that the little girl had led me to. I'd phoned Lee and he'd already checked the house out for himself. He was interested to see if its location lined up with any another clues he found on his current investigation. He promised that he'd get back to me as soon as he found anything. I knew he would. I'd just have to be patient.

I arrived at my hotel around 6.00 pm on the Sunday evening. Lisa had left a message to say that I'd be staying Melbourne and wouldn't be flying on to another destination. Banking on that being the situation I'd arranged to go out to dinner with friends at a favourite Thai restaurant in South Melbourne. I was back at my hotel by 10.00 pm so I could prepare for the next day's filming and tune into the case through the victim's date of birth which Lisa had given me. Giving me a date of birth was allowed because according to Australia's strict privacy laws, it's impossible to access information about anyone from a date of birth. I didn't spent too much time studying this particular date though, because based on who had stepped forward the most in recent days, I was pretty sure the case I was about to work on concerned a spirit I knew as Sarah.

I turned the light off at 10.30 pm, but the spiritual chatter going on in my head was so constant that I didn't get any sleep. And unlike the Mersina Case where I got by on adrenalin, this time I *did* feel the worse for wear when I fronted the camera at 9.00 am. Sarah was still the strongest energy. And equal second were Cathy or Carol, Lochie and the little Chinese girl.

'Has anyone found Lochie yet?' I asked as the crew adjusted props, camera angles and lighting.

'Not yet,' said Lisa who was sitting in her usual place just to the side of the camera. 'But we're still looking.'

The crew were son ready, and we began filming.

'Scott. We gave you a date of birth last night,' Lisa said. 'What can you tell us about the victim?'

'I definitely feel the energy of a female,' I said, 'and I have the name Sarah. Her hair is really wavy. It's down to about here,' I explained touching just below the front of my shoulders. 'Brown or brunette hair. I want to tie it up in pigtails. To me she's in her twenties but she looks younger; she could pass as a teenager, and from the energy that comes across from her I'd say she died in the early 1990's.'

Lisa handed me a photo.

Sarah McDiarmid

'Well,' I said. It's very interesting to see this photo because this is exactly as I "see" this girl.' Sarah began to show me signs and symbology. 'Now I'm seeing a sporting uniform, a train track and a train station. There's a red car associated with this case. I don't know if it's her car or someone else's, but there's a red car.' The images then became very dark and unsettling. 'I'd have to say there's a serial killer involved or someone who has killed before. As far as the train station goes, there's an Aboriginal name associated with it too. It's a K name. Kersbrook, Kanmantoo, It's got an Aboriginal sound to it. I'll figure it out. I don't come to Melbourne very often, but when I was here last I stayed at a hotel on the peninsula at Frankston, and I'm feeling that hotel when I look at this girl. So I feel the direction I need to go in to track this girl down, is towards the peninsula or towards Franklin.' Franklin was a slip of the tongue. 'Frankston!' I corrected. 'But,' I added, Franklin's a clue you know. I wanted to say Frankston and something else came out. So let's not discard the word Franklin. As for the girl, I think I know where she is. I can visualise this place, but I have to find it. So I have to let her lead me there.'

As the crew packed up ready for us to hit the road, James sat quietly with his laptop in a corner of the room.

'I've found him!' James suddenly exclaimed. 'I found Lochie!'

James turned his laptop towards me so I could see what he'd found. I got up from my chair to get a closer look. 'That's him!' I said on seeing Lochie's Matt Damon looks, chiselled jaw, and piercing stare. 'What's his name?'

James read from the screen. 'Nathan McLaughlin. And Scott, remember when you said you thought he was from the north, like around Mildura?'

'Yep.'

'Well, he's from a little further north than Mildura.'
'Where's he from?' I asked.
'The Northern Territory!'

Nathan McLaughlin

Eighteen-year-old Nathan McLaughlin is believed to have left his home in Moil, Northern Territory either on the evening of 17 March 1994, or early the next morning. He was riding a grey/silver/black racing bike and wearing shorts, T-shirt and thongs. He is believed to have been carrying or wearing a long-sleeved American army camouflage jacket. Nathan's bike was later found a short distance from Moil near the suburb of Berrimah.

Trying to focus on Lochie and Sarah at the same time was difficult, and as I waited in the downstairs car park for the crew to load the van, out of earshot I quietly spoke to Lochie who was now standing beside Sarah in spirit.

'What is it, Lochie?' I asked. 'What is it you want me to know?'

Lochie didn't say anything. He just stood there smiling, surrounded by spiritual blue light.

Lisa walked over to me. 'We're ready to go,' she said.

'Lochie's coming across really strong!' I said. 'Is he one of the cases we're doing?' As soon as I asked the question I realised that I shouldn't have. So caught up in wanting to satisfy Lochie's need to be heard, I'd stepped over the *Sensing Murder* secrecy policy.

'Can't tell you,' Lisa whispered. 'Sorry.'

Once we were on our way I decided it was time to reveal some other names.

'Aside from Sarah, I have another young woman in spirit. She's either Cathy or Carol, and I feel that was murdered and found, and that Sarah was murdered and is missing.'

About ten minutes out of Melbourne, Sarah's energy suddenly weakened and other spirits energy became stronger, which rattled me because I began to doubt whether I was leading the film crew in the right direction. Lisa noticed my confused expression.

'Something wrong Scott?' she asked.

As Lisa asked that Sarah's energy returned to being the strongest again.

'Ah no,' I said with relief. 'I had some people in spirit swapping positions, almost queue jumping, but Sarah's still leading the way.'

'Can't be easy for you to sort it all out,' Lisa mused.

'No, it's not,' I confirmed, and I settled back to focus on where Sarah wanted me to go.

As we drove towards Frankston I drew some sketches of what I was looking for. The first image Sarah showed me was a train station, train line and a pedestrian overpass.

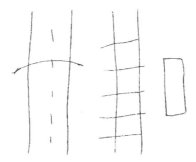

The second sketch was of a golf course; tennis club and rubbish dump located next to each other.

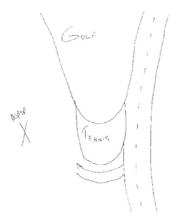

We passed a sign that said Seaford. With no-one else in the van familiar with this part of the peninsula, it went unnoticed that the driver then took a wrong turn and was heading southeast towards Langwarrin instead of directly south to Frankston.

'Where are we going?' James eventually asked, as the landscape didn't look familiar to his previous visit when he was checking out locations for the case.

'I think I took a wrong turn,' the driver confessed.

'So where are we?' James asked as we all peered out the windows.

'I'd say we're almost at Langwarrin,' came the embarrassed reply.

'It doesn't matter,' said James. 'We'll take a quick pit stop at Langwarrin and then get back on the road to Frankston.'

Five minutes later the van stopped in Langwarrin's main shopping centre car park. We all got out to stretch our legs in the mild, blue sky, autumn day.

James patted me on the shoulder. 'How's the spiritual energy going?' he asked.

'It's fine,' I said. 'I still pick up on a train line very strongly. There's got to be one around here somewhere. Once I find that, it should all fall into place.'

'Well,' said James. 'Hold on to that thought. We'll be on our way soon.'

'Scott, do you have any thoughts about the Azaria Chamberlain Case?' asked the cammo out of the blue. It was a casual question asked while we had a few minutes of time to pass.

Michael Chamberlain, his wife Lindy and their three children, left Mount Isa, Queensland in August 1980 and drove to Ayers Rock for a camping holiday. Two month old Azaria Chamberlain disappeared on the night of 17 August 1980. Her mother, Lindy, reported Azaria had been sleeping in her bassinette in the family tent, and had been taken by a dingo. Three hundred people formed a human chain during the night and searched the sand dunes near the camp site. Despite this, Azaria Chamberlain was never found. One week later, Victorian tourist, Wallace Goodwin, discovered Azaria's heavily blood-stained singlet and jumpsuit.

The initial Coroner's inquest into the Azaria Case was opened on

15 December 1980 before Mr. Denis Barritt, SM. On 20 February 1981, in the first ever live telecast of Australian court proceedings, Mr. Barritt reported that the likely cause was a dingo attack, and that subsequent to the attack, Azaria's body was taken from the dingo and disposed of by an unknown method by persons unknown.

Police and prosecutors were sceptical that a dingo could be responsible, and they were arguably under pressure to find a credible human culprit for the child's disappearance, so they moved for a further inquest. This second investigation, was held eight months later in September. Dr James Cameron of the London Hospital Medical College conducted ultra-violet investigations of the jumpsuit Azaria had been wearing on the night she disappeared. He concluded that Azaria had been killed with a pair of scissors and held by a small adult hand until she stopped bleeding.

Lindy and Michael Chamberlain were tried and convicted of Azaria's murder in 1982. The Chamberlians made several unsuccessful appeals, but eventually new evidence led to their release.

'Do you think that a dingo took her?' the cammo asked.

'Yeah I do,' I answered. 'But a dingo didn't eat Azaria. Dingoes don't eat people; they're not that fond of human flesh. A dingo might have had a bit of a play with her, but that's all. I believe that somebody local to the area found Azaria after the dingo took her, panicked as to what the repercussions of such an event would mean to their livelihood, and disposed of the body, but not the jumpsuit Azaria was wearing. The jumpsuit was deliberately discarded away from Azaria's body to lead people in the wrong direction. The jumpsuit was found, Azaria wasn't, and the finger pointing and the accusations escalated!'

'So you believe Lindy Chamberlain is innocent?' the cammo asked.

'Lindy Chamberlain was *always* innocent!' I clarified.

Shortly afterwards we were back in the van and on our way again, heading along a main road towards Frankston. We passed a sign that said East Frankston.

'There has to be a train line and train station behind these homes and shops somewhere,' I said. 'I feel it so strongly!'

I then started trying to sort out the jumbled name of the train station that I was looking for. I knew the train station started with a K, and I'd played around with all sorts of variants, none of which seemed correct.

We drove through an intersection and passed a road sign that said McClelland Drive. All I really took notice of was the word McClelland so I referred to it as street instead of its proper title of "Drive".

'Those lights that we just went through, that was McClelland Street,' I said tapping on the window of the van. That's important. Remember McClelland Street. We have to come back that. And when I say the name McClelland, I feel the golf course or the tennis club, so maybe it's worthwhile going back there later and seeing if there's a golf club and a tennis club on that road.'

As we drove on I figured that the driver's mistake of going to Langwarrin was going to turn out to be a good thing because McClelland Drive was probably a road that we wouldn't have crossed if we'd gone the "right" way. I smiled. The driver supposedly knew the area well. Maybe Sarah had confused his thoughts for a moment and steered him the "wrong" way so that I'd find McClelland!

I wouldn't be surprised.

Because I said Franklin instead of Frankston a couple more times in casual conversations, Lisa searched the Frankston area in the street directory for anything Franklin. She found a Franklin Court, and we checked it out. There two things that drew my attention in Franklin Court; a house, and an area behind the house.

In July 1990, when Sarah disappeared, there was a community correction centre only metres from Franklin Court. This centre supervised offenders who were on parole. Because of privacy laws the private investigators could not obtain documents of who attended the facility in 1990.

Lisa noted the location, and we drove on to the centre of Frankston so that I could get my spiritual bearings.

'Well I kind of feel that we've gone too far!' I said looking out the window and feeling completely lost. 'I have no sense of direction here, and I almost feel that now we're at Frankston that I've missed what I'm looking for. I'd like to follow the train line back to Seaford because I think we've come too far.' I then gestured with my hands. 'If Seaford is here, and Frankston is here, I want to be here, right in the middle somewhere.'

We were on our way again, and at that moment I almost felt like saying: Come one guys. Forget it. This is too hard. Let's go home! The level of secrecy being maintained throughout filming was also starting to annoy me. There was never a nod or a yes that I was on the right track. I just assumed that because filming a TV series costs shit loads of money that if I wasn't on the right track they'd tell me.

Was Sarah the girl's name?

Was K something the name of the train station?

Was there a train station?

Was there a red car?

Was the red car found?

Was the girl missing?

Was I going the right way?

The novelty of starting each case from scratch without knowing what the case was had certainly begun to wear out its welcome. It was like being under the pressure of doing end of year exams without knowing what the subjects were *and* not being able to study for them!

As the van cruised up a highway, I battled on.

'I'm getting a much stronger feeling now that we're heading in the right direction,' I said. And the K name is strong around here. I just have to find it. It's a train station. It's got to be a train station!'

I finally saw a train line running alongside the busy road which we were travelling on, and then ahead I could see a pedestrian overpass.

'There's the overpass!' I said excitedly, referring to the sketches I'd drawn earlier. 'It's around here somewhere!' Sarah's energy was now bubbling over like a saucepan of soup left on high on the stove. At that moment a train station came into my line of sight and then a sign that said, Kananook.

'Oh fuck there it is!' I blurted with relief, the elusive K name now solved. Kananook,' I said. 'No wonder I had trouble trying to figure it out. It's not a word I use every day!'

Cars were parked on the side of the road between the train station and me, and out of twenty cars of various colours, there was only one that was painted red.

'And there's a red car!' I said. 'She was driving a car like that!'

As it turned out, the car I was looking at was almost the same shape and size as Sarah's much earlier model car. While the crew filmed the necessary shots, Lisa finally confirmed that the girl in the case we were working on was indeed named Sarah!

Around 10.00 pm on 11 July 1990, Sarah McDiarimid caught a night train home from the city with some workmates. They travelled with her as far as Bonbeach where they got off, leaving Sarah to go on to Kananook. Ironically Sarah would normally have caught a taxi home and not caught a late train, but as she was travelling with friends most of the way this particular night she felt comfortable to catch the late train. Sarah got off at Kananook; an area frequented by drug users and small-time drug traffickers. It was a cold winter's night and she walked into a poorly lit car park towards her car, which would have been one of the few cars left. At her car she was accosted and assaulted leaving a large bloodstain on the ground next to her car. Her body was then taken across to a grass verge and shrubbery adjacent to where her car was parked and it was left on the grass for a considerable amount of time. Where Sarah was taken after that is a mystery. Police looked in drains, up and down the Kananook Creek, beaches, vacant land, parkland, anywhere a body could be conceivably hidden. But Sarah was never found.

From where I was standing on the overpass that crossed the train tracks at Kananook I began to get flustered by a bombardment of spiritual images. So much information was being fed to me from spirit that I realised I was receiving information from two or three cases instead of just one. I sighed, knowing that I'd just have to fly by the seat of my pants and sort it all through as I went! Experience had always been my greatest teacher, and I felt certain the process wouldn't let me down now!

'Have you had enough time to think about things?' Lisa asked.

'Couldn't give me a few more days could you?' I jested.

'You'll be fine!' Lisa said patting my arm.

Everyone took their positions behind the camera, and I explained what I thought had happened to Sarah.

'I believe Sarah got off the train at night, walked up the stairs along the overpass and down the stars to where her car was car parked. When she reached her car she was attacked with robbery as a motive at first. But things got out of hand.' The image of a tennis racquet and its strings flashed in my mind. 'She must have been coming home from sport.'

'What happened when Sarah was attacked?' Lisa asked.

'At first she was strangled. I can see hands around her throat. Then I see a knife. She was injured here and taken elsewhere. Her car and other items were here, but she's gone!' I surveyed the train station and surrounding area from my vantage point on the overpass. 'Someone definitely saw something and he hasn't come forward,' I said. I looked to Lisa. 'Can I be really honest?'

'Of course,' said Lisa. 'Always say everything you feel no matter what it is.

'Okay. Well there was a young guy in amongst the trees at the end of that car park that night who was getting a blowjob from another bloke. The young guy was seventeen or eighteen years old. He saw something. The other bloke didn't really see anything because he was … well …', and I paused as I thought of the best way to be tasteful, ' … he was on his knees facing the other way. That guy ran away, but the young guy, he saw a lot of what happened, but he's never come forward because he's too embarrassed!'

I went on to describe the young man; name him, and drew an identikit picture of him later that day. The private investigator found that a young man by the name I gave lived only a few streets away from Kananook at the time Sarah disappeared. Now in his early thirties and still living with his parents in the same house, the man couldn't be interviewed by the private investigator because he was overseas backpacking.

'I also can't get the name Ronald out of my head,' I said. 'And Lisa, it's a different Ronald to the one you and I know of.'

I was referring to the Executive Producer's father, Ronald, the first sprit who had stepped forward to me before we started filming. This new Ronald *wasn't* him!

'I believe that the name Ronald also refers to one of perpetrators in the Sarah Case: Ron, Don, Ronny, Donny, Ronald or Donald. Can be first or last name. It would also be worthwhile taking notice of anyone who can remember seeing a cream coloured Commodore that used to frequent Kananook around the time that Sarah disappeared as well. It's an early eighties model, and it had a rattly exhaust at the back that used to rattle and blow out a bit of smoke. I also have the number 186. Whether it's a house number, part of a telephone number, or part of a registration number, I'm not sure.'

I'd later be told that 186 was the address where serial killer Paul Denyer lived just up the road from Kananook.

I paused as a number of people on the other side wanted my attention, which prompted me to say …

'There's more than just one tragic murder that's taken place here. It's quite an overpowering feeling. Another young lady was taken from around here!'

Debbie Fream was abducted by Paul Denyer less than 500 metres from where I was standing. Another of Denyer's victims, Natalie Russell, was also murdered less than a kilometre from Kananook.

I continued with what I felt.
'I'm also seeing a yellow car, like an old Datsun or Toyota, an early model Japanese car.'

The yellow car was Paul Denyer's.

Feeling that I'd exhausted all the clues I was going to pick up on at that location, it was time to move on. 'I'd like to go back to McClelland,' I said. 'There's something else I'm looking for, and it's either a recycling station or a rubbish dump. I'd like to check that out.'

Lisa remained in charge of the street directory and compared one of my sketches to what she had in front of her as we made our way back to McClelland Drive. The sketch was accurate in outlining the Frankston City Council Recycling and Waste Disposal Centre, the Frankston East Tennis Club, and a golf club – all of which were located on McClelland Drive!

As we turned off McClelland Drive down a side road toward the gates of the recycling centre it also dawned on me that there could be a spiritual link between McDiarmid and McClelland. Was the Mc in both names a simple, obvious, spiritual clue?

As I stood outside the recycling centre the crew resumed filming.

'This is like a dumping ground,' I said! 'There's more than one person buried around here, there's someone through there too!' I said pointing to a dirt road amongst some very tall trees. 'A man,' I clarified. 'But as for Sarah I feel that she was taken inside the recycling centre, and dumped in the north-eastern corner. I also feel that the man who took Sarah was somewhat overweight, young, with dark hair, and liked to strangle and use a knife. The energy of this person was so strong around Kananook that I felt he used to frequent it, or live nearby. He was very familiar with it.'

At that moment I couldn't get the song: "Take Me Home Country Roads", by John Denver out of my head.

'Why am I thinking of John Denver?' I asked. 'Maybe the perpetrators name is John,' I suggested. But immediately that didn't feel right. 'No it's not John,' I said. I'm actually now picking up on a P name: Peter, Patrick, Paul' The energy around the name Paul was much stronger so I made my decision. 'It's Paul!' I announced. I then had a thought. 'Didn't I say the name Paul during the Mersina Case?'

Lisa didn't answer my question. Instead, she asked one. 'Do you feel Paul is free or in jail?'

'Sarah's telling me he's in jail!' I answered.

Paul Denyer killed three women in around Kananook. He was questioned by police but denied killing Sarah, and there was no evidence to link him to Sarah's disappearance.

I flew home and that was supposed to be the end of it for me as far as the Sarah Case went. But something wasn't right! When I spoke to Lisa by phone a few days later, I told her that I thought I might be wrong about who had taken Sarah.

'I think I've mixed up the cases,' I told her. 'I think I've mistaken the John Denver Paul guy for someone else. Can I go back to Kananook and sort out what I'm feeling?'

Ten days later I was back with the film crew in the car park at Kananook.

'The man I nicknamed John Denver Paul,' I said. 'You obviously know who I'm referring to. Is it known by the police that he used to frequent the station on some kind of level, because I feel his car here and I feel him here. Can you confirm that to me?'

'Yes he used to frequent here. Yes he's known to the police,' Lisa answered 'He used to live less than 300 metres from Kananook Station.'

'Did he drive a cream coloured Commodore?' I asked.

'No, a yellow Toyota.'

Oh my god, I thought. That explains the yellow car I'd been picking up on. When Lisa told me that the penny dropped and a mind swell of jumbled images and feelings fell into place. I'd been picking up on two different cases that occurred in and around Kananook; the first being what Lisa told me were known as the Frankston Murders, and the second being Sarah's disappearance! Both cases had spiritually overlapped. I'd assumed that all the information I'd picked up on was just about one case: Sarah's! But it *wasn't*. Because I'd felt Paul Denyer's energy around Kananook, I assumed that he was the one who'd taken Sarah. But as I delved further on a psychic level, I couldn't make Paul Denyer fit the Sarah Case! If he had been involved, I don't believe that Sarah would still be missing. I believe she would've been found very quickly,' (as per Denyer's other victims). 'I still felt the name Paul is relevant to the Sarah Case. I felt Sarah was attacked by a gang of people that the names Paul, Ronny, and Donny were associated with. I also feel there was a woman involved. This gang used to hang around Kananook. One person didn't take Sarah. There was a gang of them!'

Private investigators confirmed there was a Donny at Kananook on the night Sarah disappeared. The police had never made Donny's name public. His name didn't appear on the electoral role or any public record. He and other people of his nature go to incredible lengths not to be found. The private investigators found him.

Notorious prostitute Jodi Jones used to hang out at the Kananook train station with a gang of male drug addicts. She and Donny knew each other. Jodi Jones had an alibi that she stayed at the home of a female friend on the night Sarah disappeared. Private investigators found the friend who said that she could not be totally sure that Jodi stayed with her on the night Sarah disappeared. There were also other discrepancies in Jodi's alibi. During a stay in jail, Jodi Jones admitted to a friend that she killed Sarah and that the police would never find the body. Jodi Jones died from an overdose a year after Sarah disappeared.

Another witness claimed she saw Jodi and Donny at the station shortly after 10.00 pm. She says they followed a girl matching the description of Sarah and attacked her. The witness heard Jodi Jones scream out, 'She's dead what have you done, she's dead!' Soon after Sarah disappeared, the witness received a threatening letter telling her to keep her mouth shut and she retracted her statement to police. When private investigators tracked this witness down she refused to speak to them.
According to private investigators Paul was 'Paul the dwarf'. Some years after Sarah disappeared Paul gassed himself to death by connecting a pipe to the exhaust of his car. Paul the dwarf drove an

old cream or white Holden sedan. Witness say a car matching that description was seen at Kananook on the night Sarah disappeared.

The northeast corner of the recycling centre is now reclaimed land with a ground level twenty metres higher than it was in 1990! The area was an active area of the tip when Sarah disappeared. In 1990 a supervisor was present to direct people to the appropriate landfill areas where they could dispose of their rubbish. Police considered looking for Sarah at the Frankston tip but felt as there was no real link to the tip that digging it up would be like looking for a needle in a haystack, and that resources would be better spent elsewhere.

One way of detecting buried objects is by using ground-penetrating radar or GPR which detects disturbances in the soil, but as all the soil was disturbed, GPR is not an option. If a body had been dumped there in 1990 Council says it would now be twenty metres down under concrete and building waste, plus green and putrescible wastes, making any excavation extremely dangerous and not a viable option.

Before this episode went to air a computer technician created an identikit picture of what I felt the main person who took Sarah looked like.

'Donny'

After this episode aired, viewers from Western Australia and Victoria came forward saying that the identikit picture looked exactly like a friend of theirs whose name was Donny. They supplied the same surname for Donny and said that he used to live in Western Australia, but went to Melbourne in 1989 and lived in Frankston.

With filming of the Sarah Case completed, Lisa was able to tell me other details about Paul Denyer and the infamous Frankston Murders. Once I learned that he lived so close to Kananook and used to hang out at the train station, it reaffirmed why I'd confused his activities with what had happened to Sarah. And while Lisa and James had recognised why I was getting confused early on, because of the *Sensing Murder* secrecy policy they couldn't tell me at the time.

Chapter 9

ANY CLUES?

During my next week off from *Sensing Murder* I caught up with some friends who live on a large property in the country right away from it all. I love to go there and share a meal and a few laughs under a brilliant night sky of stars. Around 11.00 pm I bid my friends goodbye and drove away from their property along a six kilometre private dirt road. As I neared the end of the dirt road, I saw the little girl standing next to a bush, and as she had a habit of showing up when I least expected it, seeing her didn't surprise me. I parked my car and got out, and when I looked to where the little girl had been standing, she was gone … or was she? I could still feel her energy.

I leant against my car, folded my arms across my chest, and after a few patient moments I noticed her again. She was now standing amongst some long rye grass on the other side of the dirt road. She then giggled and ran around like a kid in a playground. I smiled. I'd seen her play hide-and-seek before. Even ghosts liked to have fun! She merrily ran around for a couple of minutes and then came to a stop just in front of me. I noticed that she wasn't puffing or panting.

'I know you from somewhere, don't I?' I said. 'On the TV … radio … in the newspapers … I know I've seen you but I just can't figure out where!' I studied the little girl. She stood there looking at me, spiritual blue light shimmering around her. 'You wouldn't like to give me a clue would you?' I asked. 'I mean any help would be gratefully appreciated!' She continued to stand there in silence, a coy expression on her face. 'You actually remind me of my friend Jenny,' I said.

In an instant my mind sailed back to when I was twelve-years-old. 'Jenny lived next door and we spent a lot of time together. One night she visited me in a dream and said goodbye, kissing me on the cheek.' I sighed. 'The next day she and her family were killed in a head-on crash on a country road. I know you're not Jenny,' I said to the little girl, 'but you remind me of her.'

I put my hands snugly into my jeans pockets. 'Is Grant with you tonight?' I asked. Grant Beaumont also liked to run around free as the wind. I checked to see if he was anywhere in sight, but he wasn't.

The little girl took a few steps closer to me and was now only about a metre away. 'Any clues to your name?' I asked. I didn't expect any, but it was worth a shot. I waited a few more moments, but she offered nothing on that particular secret. 'Okay, well if you don't want to tell me your name at least tell me what you want, why you've picked me to visit.'

The little girl still didn't answer me so I decided to draw our meeting to a close.

'Look, I'm a little tired and I've got a long drive ahead of me, so I'm going to head off now,' I said. 'I'll see you next time.'

I got into my car, closed the door and looked to where the little girl had been standing. She was gone!

The overpowering heat of the Pilbara transformed itself into desert chill once the sun went down, it's unrelenting glare replaced by a veil of night. In any direction I looked a thin band of deep blue marked the horizon, silhouetting the craggy peaks of distant hills.

Sitting on the dusty ground, I watched a crackling campfire glow with an orange flame as it shot sparks and tendrils of smoke upwards. Above, in a cloudless sky, the moon was yet to rise and the numerous stars of the Milky Way seemed closer, twinkling light of varying intensities from their distant places in the universe.

An Aboriginal elder sat by the campfire. He was true yin and yang; a mass of white curly hair and jet-black skin. I noticed a figure hiding amongst some rocks behind him. It was the little girl in the pink dress. The elder noticed that I was observing something and turned to see what it was. His movement started the little girl and she looked like she was about to make a run for it when …

'Don't be afraid little one,' the elder said. He was speaking in his native dialect, but I was hearing him in English. He beckoned her with a wave of his hand and a big grin full of white teeth. 'The desert is your home!'

The little girl came out from behind the rocks. She walked over to the elder and he took her by the hand.

I woke up. How many times had I had that dream? Close to ten times, but it had never gone into so much detail! Usually the dream stopped *without* me seeing the little girl behind the rocks. But this time I saw her, and now that I had, the repetitive nature of the dream didn't so much become clear to me, but at least I understood why I'd been having it so often. The little girl was in the dream because it was a clue to who she was.

The first time I'd had the dream was a few years earlier during a trip to Karratha in the north and remote Pilbara region of Western Australia. "The desert is your home. That's what the elder had said to the little girl. I wondered if she'd been murdered or gone missing in the Pilbara? I rang and checked with my friends in Karratha, Dampier and Port Headland, but no one could recall something like that happening anywhere in the region in recent years.

I'd drawn another blank, and remained none the wiser as to who she was. But I wasn't deterred. One way or another I'd figure out the mysterious real-life identity of the little girl.

Chapter Ten

CHINESE GIRL

I flew up from the ground and saw a small, boutique type shopping centre with umbrellas where you could have lunch and coffee outdoors. In the distance behind the shopping centre suburbia diminished and gave way to rolling green hills. I came down to land in the shopping centre's car park, and once my feet were on the ground a little Chinese girl walked out from behind one of the buildings and came over to me.

'Will you help me?' she softly asked.

'Of course,' I said.

The little Chinese girl looked over her shoulder as if she were checking to see if the coast was clear. There was no one there, not that I could see anyway.

'I have a name to tell you.'

I nodded. 'Okay.'

The little Chinese girl was about to tell me when …

Someone noisily handling some breakfast trays in the hotel hallway outside my door abruptly woke me.

'Bastard!' I sighed referring to the noisemaker outside. I'd had this dream a few times now and this was the closest I'd gotten to the little Chinese girl saying the name that she wanted to tell me.

I glanced at the bedside clock. 7.30 am. Time to get up.

I couldn't stop yawning when I fronted the camera at 9.00 am to begin filming the next case.

'Another sleepless night?' Lisa asked.

'Unfortunately,' I said flatly as I scratched my tired eyes.

I was sitting in my regular chair as lights and camera angles were set up around me.

'Can I tell you about Lochie?' Lisa asked.

I leant to the side and shielded my eyes from a light that was shining in my face so I could see Lisa properly. 'There's news?' I asked with anticipation.

'We contacted his family and they thanked us very much but declined our offer to feature his case on *Sensing Murder*.'

'Oh, well, that's a pity,' I said. 'For his energy to be so strong he really wanted to be noticed and ...' I stopped mid sentence as something caught my eye. Lisa, followed my gaze.

'Is it Lochie?' Lisa asked.

'No,' I said. 'There's a little girl who's been visiting me for a while. She's standing by the camera just to your left.'

The soundie was just about to step into that area and recoiled when I said that. 'Shit!' he said, 'did I step on her?'

Nervous laughter filled the room.

'No, she's gone now,' I said. 'You can stand there.'

'Who is she?' Lisa asked.

'That's the million dollar question,' I said. 'I haven't got a clue. I keep asking her tell me, but she doesn't!'

'Why do spirits do that?' asked James from the sidelines. 'Why don't they just come straight out with what they want to say?'

'Maybe they do James,' I said. 'Maybe it's *me* who's not picking up properly on what they're saying!'

When the cameras rolled a few minutes later, I started talking about the little Chinese girl.

'From the date of birth you gave me last night, I feel a person in spirit who I call the little Chinese girl. I'm not sure what happened to her yet, but I did have a dream!'

And I went on to describe my flying over the shopping centre dream, after which I put forward an interesting conundrum.

'Before we started filming I was sure at first that the little Chinese girl wanted me to north, north east of Melbourne,' I said. 'Now it's completely changed. Now she wants me to go south!'

When I said south there were some looks of surprise amongst those in the room. I read those looks as one of two possibilities. Either we were meant to go northeast and they were surprised I now wanted to go south, or we were meant to go south all along and I'd locked into the correct direction at the last minute! Whatever the reason, as I'd grown to appreciate, the day would reveal the truth soon enough!

Melbourne was putting on its best weather. For an autumn day in May it was blue skies and twenty-three degrees which brought up one of a number of conversations in the van about how desperately Victoria needed some decent rain. As discussions ensued about water restrictions and low reservoir levels, my attention was being taken by another young spirit stepping forward.

'What suburb is this?' I asked.

'Prahran.'

'Has a little boy gone missing from around here?'

'Who are you picking up on? Lisa asked.

'I'm not sure,' I said. 'But his energy's really coming in strong as we're heading this way.

'There's not been a little boy disappear from around here as far as I know,' Lisa said.

'I can't think of anyone either,' said James. 'How old is he?'

'I'd say seven or eight. He reminds me of the kid who plays Harry Potter – dark hair, sharp features.'

'Is the little boy wearing glasses like Harry Potter?' Lisa asked.

'No.'

And as for the name of the actor was who played Harry Potter, we all had mental blanks. It took about fifteen seconds of jolting bad memories before someone finally said, Daniel Radcliffe.

'Maybe this little boy's name is Daniel I said, following the obvious spiritual clue. But I changed my mind as soon as I said it. 'Nah, I don't get any energy from the name Daniel.'

'Harry?' Lisa suggested.

'No. I have the name Taylor. Did a little boy with the last name of Taylor disappear from around here?'

After a thoughtful five seconds and a van of shaking heads, the answer was still no.

I sighed. 'Well I don't have a clue then who he is,' I said. 'I've got so many people talking in my head, what's one more?' As best I could I pushed the energy of the little boy to one side and encouraged the energy of the little Chinese girl to be stronger. There was definitely something to the south of Melbourne that she wanted me to find. After another twenty minutes of me saying turn left, turn right, we ended up driving along the beach.

'The little Chinese girl keeps showing me my own name,' I said. 'She keeps showing me Scott. But it's not me or another person. It's a place! Is there a Scott Park or a Scott Street around here somewhere?'

Lisa took out the street directory. 'Yes there is,' she told me, but she didn't elaborate.

'Just the one location of that name near here?' I asked trying to narrow it down.

'Can't say,' said Lisa.

'That was Lisa's succinct way of telling me that I'd have to work it out for myself!

'But there *is* a Scott location or locations near here?' I asked.

'Yes.'

'Take me to the nearest one,' I said.

After Lisa had a whispered conversation with James, the van followed the curves and bends of a seaside road, with houses to my left, and the ocean to my right. Suddenly the spiritual energy from the little Chinese girl overflowed and I broke out in a sweat.

Stop the van! Stop the van!' I said loudly and very animated. Let me out!' The driver hit the brakes and abruptly pulled the van over to the kerb. Everyone piled out and I clambered out of the van dripping in perspiration as if I'd just run the Boston Marathon.

'Shit!' I exclaimed as I flicked my hands away from me. I was so covered in sweat on my face and body that it was running down my hands and dripping off the ends of my fingers. I peeled my shirt from my chest, and Lisa pulled it away from my back because the material was saturated and sticking to my skin.

'Scott are you okay?' James asked, a concerned frown covering his brow. 'What just happened?'

'I'm fine,' I assured him as I flapped the front of my shirt to let some air in. 'Now I know why I was getting confused,' I said. Everyone waited expectantly. 'I know why the little Chinese girl wanted us to go south. Because it *hasn't* been the little Chinese girl who's been leading the way!'

The glazed expressions that greeted me upon that revelation made it glaringly obvious that no one knew what the hell I was talking about. So I explained further.

'The most incredible thing just happened!' I said. 'Right up until just before we pulled over all I saw was the little Chinese girl's face, and all I felt was what I believed to be *her* energy. But all of a sudden *another* girl stepped out from behind the little Chinese girl! I thought all along that it was the little Chinese girl who was leading me here, but it's actually been the *other* girl!'

'Do you have a name on this other girl?' James asked.

'I keep seeing one of the girls from *The Sound of Music*. Oh shit, I can't

remember her name. Not the eldest one ...'

'Leisl,' Lisa prompted.

'No not her. The next one.'

'Louisa,' said Lisa filling in the gap once again.

'Yeah. I think this girl's name is Louisa.'

I wandered off on my own to dry off and gather my thoughts. It was pleasant and relaxing here by the ocean, and my shirt and skin began to dry out in the sunshine and gentle breeze. Lisa walked over to me.

'Look,' said Lisa, 'We're not too far from the "Scott" connection you were talking about. We'd like to take you near there, drop you off, and see which way the spirits want you to go.'

The van followed the seaside road for about another five minutes and then turned left into a street that took us away from the ocean. The van pulled over by a park and what looked like a school to one side, and houses on the other.

'It's over to you, Scott,' James said.

I got out of the van and stood in a regular looking suburban street. The birds were obviously enjoying the days' sunshine because there was a lot of chirping going on. As I didn't sense a particular spiritual pull to go in either direction,

I decided to start walking to the left of the van. I reached the end of the street and turned a corner, but I noticed when I did this that the energy around "Scott" began to diminish, which meant I was going the wrong way! So I turned on my heels and followed the footpath back the way I'd come. I walked past the van up to the next corner and turned left.

The word "Scott" was now flashing in my mind like a neon sign. Just up ahead was a street to the right. I looked for a street sign to tell me what its name was.

It was Scott Street!

I made my way up Scott Street and came to a halt outside one particular house at an intersection. The little Chinese girl had stepped right back now. The only person I could see was the smiling face of Louisa!

'Is this where you used to live Louisa?' I asked softly as I looked at the modest house.

The van parked a couple of houses back from where I was standing, and James and Lisa walked over to me.

'Do you know who Louisa is?' I asked Lisa.

She nodded. 'I just made a call back to the office and spoke to some of the researchers who confirmed her identity.'

'Who is she?' I asked.

'Well before we get to that,' said Lisa, 'what I need you to know is that this *isn't* one of our cases, just so that you can try and separate from it.'

'Oh,' I said a little disheartened.

Lisa put her hand on my shoulder. 'You've got no control over who comes through or when. We're learning to roll with the punches, just like you are.'

'Yeah,' I sighed. 'But what if Louisa is related to the case we're meant to be filming? What if the same person committed the crime? What if there are clues in the Louisa Case that relate to the little Chinese girl?'

'Well,' Lisa said sympathetically. 'I guess those are issues that only you can sort out!'

Louisa was a young girl called Eloise Worledge. She had led me to the seaside suburb of Beaumaris, and I was standing in front of where she used to live. In January 1976, eight-year-old Eloise was taken from her bed in the middle of the night. A torn fly screen and an open window were the main clues. Police believed it might be a red herring. Her parents were so bitterly estranged that her father, Lindsay came under police scrutiny.

Eloise Worledge

More than 250 police joined the search and canvassed 6,000 homes in the Beaumaris area with a prepared list of questions. They were able to log 200 suspicious incidents in the street and nearby area that occurred on the night Louise was abducted. Police interviewed more than 100 family and extended family members in Australia and overseas, more than 200 friends and associates of the family, neighbours and work colleagues. Police looked at ten general types of suspects. Known sex offenders in Melbourne's south-east, any sex offenders within Australia involved in child abductions or who broke into houses, known prowlers in the area, local service providers, babysitters, tradesmen, door-to-door salesmen, staff and parents at the Beaumaris Primary School, and government agencies with any contact with the family. In the end police had no suspects whatsoever, and the Eloise Worledge Case remains unsolved.

In 2003 Eloise's father took a police lie detector test to dispel rumours that he was involved with her disappearance. He took the test after police reopened the case, but the findings of the polygraph were inconclusive. A Melbourne coroner was also told that vital

crime scene evidence and police records into the case were lost, and
that this had hampered police investigations back in 1976.

Standing with Lisa outside the house where Eloise used to live. I had a sudden thought. 'Whatever happened to Eloise is similar to what happened to the little Chinese girl,' I said. 'That's why they're together on the other side. They have a common bond.'

'Does the little Chinese girl want you to stay here or go somewhere else?' Lisa asked again.

'She wants me to go north east like I originally thought.'

'Scott,' James said, 'Because time's running short now, we need to get you to the area where we think you need to be because depending on traffic, it could take up to an hour to get there from here.'

James was right! It did take almost an hour, and just after we'd passed a road sign that said Doncaster, we pulled over and parked to the side of a busy main road.

The little Chinese girl gave me a few clues.

'Okay,' I began. 'Well obviously I'm looking for the shopping centre that I saw in my dream. I also keep thinking about James Hardy wines. So maybe there's a James Hardy wine centre or a bottle department located at the shopping centre that's important to find.' I looked up and down the busy road, then left and right at the businesses and shops that lined it. 'Keep going straight ahead,' I instructed. The van pulled away from the kerb and we were on our way again. 'Which direction are we heading in?' I asked.

'East,' said Lisa.

We approached some traffic lights and a large Westfield shopping centre loomed in front of us on the other side of the intersection.

'I need to get my bearings at the lights,' I said. 'The little Chinese girl is telling me that we need to change direction.'

'Is that the shopping centre you saw in your dream?' Lisa asked, referring to the Westfield

'No. The one I saw isn't as big. It's single story with umbrellas and tables and chairs outside where you can drink coffee. I feel to get there that we need to turn left at those lights just ahead,' I said. Which we did, and the little Chinese girl's energy doubled. 'I'm looking for an area that's newer than where we were back there with Eloise,' I said. 'We're looking for an area that has newer and bigger houses, bigger blocks of land, more opulent!' We drove north for a couple of minutes and crossed a couple of intersections. 'Can we pull over here?' I asked.

We parked and I got my bearings again.

'I think she used to live over there somewhere,' I said pointing to the left hand side of the van. 'And I reckon the shopping centre I'm looking for is that way,' I said pointing to the front.

We were on our way again and the road widened at an intersection where a number of main roads veered off in different directions. In the distance suburbia gave way to rolling green hills.

'That's it, that's it!' I exclaimed. 'Those are the hills I saw in my dream! The shopping centre has to be around here somewhere!' I had to quickly decide which way I wanted to go. 'At the next set of lights, turn left. Let's have a look along there.'

The van turned and we entered an undulating and hilly area. Houses were built on either side of the road and judging from their appearance, this was the kind of opulent suburb I was looking for.

'I have a Seppelts Road,' I said. 'Does that mean anything to anyone?' No one said anything. 'She lived around here,' I said again looking to both sides of the van. 'What's that street up there just on the right?' I asked. 'Is that Seppelts?' Travelling along the main road the driver had nowhere to stop now but cruised past the right hand road as slowly as he could so that I could read the street sign: Serpells Road. 'She lived down there,' I said confidently.

'Yes,' Lisa confirmed.

'So we *are* looking for a little Chinese girl?' I asked.

'Yes. Do you get a name at all?'

'Not yet,' I answered.

Before long I was leading the film crew again, looking for a shopping centre that had rolling hills behind it. We turned left, turned right, seemingly went around and around in circles, but no shopping centre. I kept thinking about James Hardy wines. It had to be a clue. Frustrated that we had less than an hour of daylight and that we didn't seem to be making much progress, I made a suggestion.

'Why doesn't someone call information and see if there's a James Hardy wine centre around here. Maybe there's one in the shopping centre that we're looking for.'

The van idled on the side of the road as Lisa made the call. But her efforts came up with zero.

'There is no James Hardy wine centre around here,' she told me.

'Then I don't know,' I said. 'I don't know what else to suggest. Until I find the shopping centre, no other clues will come through.'

The decision was made to continue driving. Suddenly I got a real spiritual buzz, and my internal compass started leaning towards a particular direction. I followed its lead.

'Turn left up ahead here,' I pointed, 'at that roundabout.'

We turned left and were still in suburbia with no sign of a shopping centre or anything that the name James Hardy might apply to. The road was about to fork in two different directions.

'Left or right Scott?' James asked urgently. 'There's someone tailgating right up our bum!'

'Left!' I said.

So the van veered left and after passing a couple more houses low and behold, on the right hand side of the van …

'There's the shopping centre!' I said excitedly. 'That's the one!' and the van pulled over to the side of the road.

'What street is this?' I asked.

'James Street!' Lisa announced. 'I feel like an idiot,' she added. ' I didn't see it in the street directory.'

It was now around 4.30 pm, and we were at Templestowe Village Shopping Centre, which looked exactly as I'd described it from my dream. Lots of boutique shops and from a particular vantage point, yes there were rolling hills in the distance behind it. It was here Lisa showed me the photos of two girls, Sharon Wills and Nicola Lynas. Then I was shown a photo of the little Chinese girl and told her name; Karmein Chan.

Karmein Chan

"Mr Cruel" is the name given to an unknown Australian murderer and rapist who attacked his victims in suburban Melbourne during the 1980's and 90's. Police believe Mr Cruel is responsible for the abduction of ten-year-old Sharon Wills from Ringwood in 1988. Wills was held prisoner and assaulted for eighteen hours before being dressed in plastic rubbish bags and dropped off at a school in Bayswater.

Later, thirteen-year-old Nicola Lynas disappeared from her Canterbury home in 1990 in similar circumstances. Lynas remained missing for 50 hours. Mr Cruel only released her after taking meticulous steps to avoid leaving identifying evidence. Police believe he's responsible for as many as twelve attacks on children over a ten-year period (1982-1992).

Mr Cruel is last believed to have struck in 1991, when thirteen-year-old Templestowe schoolgirl Karmein Chan was abducted from her luxury family home. He cut a fly screen in the lounge room and took Karmein, leaving her two sisters behind. Mr Cruel left his trademark red herring of leaving a message. He spray painted the words "More", "More to Come", and "Pay back, Asian Drug Dealer" on the bonnet and front windscreen of Mrs Chan's car.

In more recent times police have said they believe Mr Cruel is alive and well and living in Victoria. They say they know where he is and have kept tabs on the man for more than a decade. He is the prime suspect - but police don't have a strong enough case to charge him.

Serial sexual predators like Mr Cruel usually keep attacking until they are caught or die. But Commander Sprague, head of Operation Spectrum (the taskforce set up to catch the offender) believes the reason Mr Cruel has not struck again is he became scared after being tracked down and interviewed by Operation Spectrum detectives. 'I honestly think we got very, very close. So close that he stopped,' he said.

Operation Spectrum detectives know things about Mr Cruel that have not been made public. They have used this knowledge to eliminate more than 27,000 suspects. But they have not been able to rule out the prime suspect. He fits both the public and secret profiles of Mr Cruel. It was also reported that the Herald Sun newspaper had discovered that police had lost, contaminated or destroyed vital evidence that may have convicted Mr Cruel. Victoria Police Commander Dave Sprague also revealed that crucial forensic evidence might have been rendered useless as a result of the last known Mr Cruel crime scene not being sealed off as it should have been. Commander Sprague revealed he was not impressed by what he found on arriving at Karmein Chan's home within hours of her abduction. 'The crime scene was not preserved as it should have been,' he said. 'We had a lot of problems with it. Unfortunately, the initial police member in charge had set up the command post inside the house. Commander Sprague is concerned evidence that might have identified Mr Cruel was possibly destroyed in those first few vital hours.

He later discovered it was not the first time a chance to identify the kidnapper had been lost. Operation Spectrum established that Mr Cruel was almost certainly responsible for an early series of sex attacks in Melbourne's southern suburbs in the 1980's. Detectives wanted to review the evidence from those Cases. But they were bitterly disappointed to find some of the evidence had been lost.

Of particular concern was that the tape Mr Cruel had used to bind one of his victims was missing. Forensic technology has improved since those attacks in the 1980's and scientists can extract identifying characteristics from the smallest of samples. Mr Cruel's DNA may well have been on that tape because it is likely he was not as careful during those early attacks as he was in the later abductions of Sharon Wills, Nicola Lynas and Karmein Chan. 'But we will never know as the exhibit just isn't there anymore,' Commander Sprague said. 'In those days police just didn't have the supervision that they do now.'

'What can you tell me about the night Karmein disappeared?' Lisa asked me.

'That the man entered through her bedroom window, took her from her bed, back through her bedroom window, down the driveway, up the street and around the corner to where a van was waiting. Someone else was driving the van, and after Karmein was taken they momentarily stopped here at this shopping centre. Either a cleaner or a couple taking their dog for a late night walk saw the van. The main perpetrator got out and went to the back of the van to check something. Satisfied, he got back in the van and they drove away. I feel after that they went to a warehouse or somewhere that stores grains, wheat and various foodstuffs. I can also hear jets flying overhead, so maybe it's near an airport, or in a flight path to the airport.'

Suddenly both Karmein and Eloise stepped forward, and their combined spiritual energies sent me a barrage of symbols and images. My mind went into overload. I took a moment to speak to Lisa.

'There's something not right with this case,' I said.

'How so?' asked Lisa.

'Well, you keep on talking about Mr Cruel, but I can't match him up completely to what you've told me or to what I'm feeling. It's a little like when I was picking up on Paul Denyer's energy around Kananook station but it was really the gang who were the culprits. He just happened to hang around the same area! I pretty much feel the same thing now. Everyone thinks it's Mr Cruel, but I'm leaning towards thinking that it was someone else or at least that someone else was involved. Could there possibly have been a copycat? And what's the link between Karmein and Eloise? Was it the same person who took them?'

'No one knows who took Eloise,' Lisa told me. 'She was never found. As for Karmein who was found dead a year after she disappeared, it seems pretty conclusive that it was Mr Cruel. There were trademark signatures left on the scene.'

'Hmm,' I said, I hear what you're saying but there's something about Karmein's Case that's just not right. I feel there's a deeper reason why she went missing. And I don't think it was ever intended that she would be killed, but something got bungled along the way.'

As we drove back to Melbourne from Templestowe, I gazed out the van's window and took in the towering night skyline of Melbourne. Most of the buildings were lit up, making the city a spectacular sight from this side of the Yarra River. Lost in my own thoughts, I didn't take any notice of a call Lisa took on her mobile.

'Well, Scott,' said Lisa as she hung up from the call. 'The researchers at the office may have found the little boy you picked up on earlier today. They've found a Craig Taylor Ewen, and they say that he does have the sharp chiselled features of a young Daniel Radcliffe.

No one in the van reacted to what Lisa was telling me. There was silence. Not an, oh that's right, I remember him – nothing! I didn't need to be Einstein to realise that everyone's non-response meant they'd never heard of this boy!

'Where's he from?' I asked.

'Tasmania,' said Lisa.

I sat back in my seat and sighed. 'Gee,' I said. These spirits are coming in from all points of Australia aren't they!'

'But why would you pick up on Craig while we were driving through Prahran?' Lisa asked.

I pondered Lisa's question for a few moments. 'Prahran specifically?' I said. 'Perhaps someone connected to Craig's disappearance lives there now, either a perpetrator, accomplice or a witness. Maybe there's a relative of his is there. Or on the other side of the coin maybe there's no direct connection to Prahran. Maybe I was just meant to pick up on Craig's energy. Without more time to figure it out, I'm just stabbing in the dark.

Craig Ewen

Craig Ewen lived in the north of Tasmania in the suburb of East Launceston with his mother, father and two older sisters. In August 1993 ten-year-old Craig and his immediate family arranged to spend the September school holidays in Conningham, South Tasmania. Craig was last seen by his mother mid-morning on 3 September 1993. All searches of the area and enquiries to date have failed to locate any trace of Craig.

As I'd done previously on the Sarah Case, with the help of a computer animator I created an identikit picture of who I believed took Karmein. I did this when we returned to the production office around 7.00 pm.

We'd covered quite a number of kilometres on this particular case, and I was exhausted by the time I caught my 8.45 pm flight home.

The night was clear as I flew across the sky. Not a cloud to be seem. Twinkling stars above, country lights below. Some hills appeared ahead and I sailed over them effortlessly. Across the countryside I flew, and as I crested a tree-lined hill, the lights of a country town appeared ahead to my left, and the lights of a city were further on in the distance to my right. I realised as soon as I saw those lights that I'd taken this journey before. It was familiar. I veered towards an area in between the lights of the country town and the city, and I slowly descended, gently landing on a dirt road that passed in front of an older style house. No lights were on in the house. It looked ominous and foreboding.

Why am I here again? I wondered.

What is it they want me to see?

The little girl in the pink dress appeared, standing on the road between the house and me. She looked to me with sombre eyes.

'The bad people live here!' she told me sadly.

'Who are the bad people?' I asked. She stood in front of me and avoided my gaze. 'Who are the bad people?' I asked again.

As I said those words Daniel Morcombe materialised close to where the little girl was standing. The two or three photos I'd seen of Daniel always showed him with a smiling face and shorter hair. But the way I was seeing Daniel now was different to those images. His hair was longer and unkempt, and his beaming smile had made way not so much for a sad expression, but a yearning … a yearning to be found! Then I wondered what to call him. In everything I'd seen he was always Daniel. I wondered if that was too formal for him.

'Hi,' I said. 'Um, do you like to be called Daniel or Dan … or Danny?'

'With you he likes Daniel,' the little girl told me.

'Okay,' I said. 'Daniel it is!' Which was interesting. Spirits were often very formal with me when it came to their name … of course Lochie was an exception. Daniel stood quietly and immersed in spiritual blue light. 'What do you want me to know Daniel?' I asked. 'Is there something you want to tell me? Something you want your family to know?'

At that moment another spirit suddenly appeared next to Daniel. It was Nathan McLachlin or Lochie, as I called him. The little girl took hold of my hand.

'They're my friends,' she told me. 'We look after each other.'

'I'm very glad to hear that,' I said.

Lochie walked a few steps over to Daniel. They looked at each other with the familiar comfort that best mates have, and then stood side by side, watching me intently.

'So Lochie,' I said. 'You and Daniel and have become friends in spirit, just like Karmein and Eloise have. With Karmein and Eloise the common bond is they were taken from their bedrooms … maybe they were even were taken by the same person. So what's the common bond between you two?' No sooner had I asked that question when a dark figure on a noisy trail bike sped out from behind the house and headed towards Lochie and Daniel!

'Look out!' I warned.

I woke up with a start, the noise of the 737 cruising at 10,000 metres droned through my ears. An episode of *Friends* that I'd seen five or six times was playing on the TV screen in front of me, and I noticed that my dinner tray had been cleared while I was asleep. I raised my tray table and clipped it to the back of the seat in front of me. I adjusted the flow of air coming from the nozzle above me, settled back into my chair, and peered out the window. Lights far below in the darkness signalled that we were passing over a country town, and I kept watching the lights as they slowly passed below the plane.

I thought about what I'd just dreamt, what the little girl, Daniel and Lochie had shown me. I recalled from the notes that I'd read on Lochie that he'd been driving a trail bike when he'd disappeared. Daniel Morcombe was keen on motocross and had asked his parents to let him join the local motocross club at Coolum on the Sunshine Coast in Queensland. And I'd just seen a man on a trail bike race towards both these boys.

Was that the spiritual key to Lochie and Daniel's Cases? Were they trying to tell me that not only were they into motocross and trail bikes, but so were their assailants?

Chapter 11

PHILLIP ISLAND

A month into working on *Sensing Murder,* and despite my lack of sleep, I hadn't come undone at the edges because of the intensity of what I was doing. If I solved a case, that would be great. If I gave new clues that helped solve a case, also great. I figured that the only constructive way to sift through all the spiritual clues was to stop focusing on all the people talking in my head, and just centre my thoughts towards one case at a time. Otherwise it was like trying to do ten jigsaw puzzles all at once.

I was unexpectedly asked if I'd help out on a *Sensing Murder* Case that I wasn't originally scheduled to be a part of. The psychics working on the case had come up with a few things, but not enough. My role was to try and come up with more clues. With broadcast deadlines looming, and time running out to complete the case, the producers had decided to break the format so that I could help!

'We're hoping that if we hand you the case notes that you might be able to come up with a psychic determination,' Lisa told me. 'We'll be very up front about it on the show, and the audience will be told what's happened.'

I flew into Melbourne to film my part on the Phillip Island Case. I felt more relaxed not having to figure out what the case was, it was like had a big weight had been lifted off my shoulders. Lisa waited with me in the downstairs car park as the crew filled the van with their equipment. It was a blustery winter's day, and the sky was a mass of grey clouds while drizzling rain fell sideways because the wind was so strong.

'Not the best day for filming, I said.

'No,' agreed Lisa as she gripped her folder of notes tightly. 'Although when it's overcast like this the light is very filtered,' she added, 'so without the glare of the sun on your face you'll come up on screen looking like a film star.'

'Will I get paid like a film star?' I jested.

Lisa smiled. 'What was it like to have the case notes and not have to start from scratch?'

'It was like someone turned a light on!' I said. 'As I read the case notes I formed an immediate opinion of what I believed happened.'

'Is anyone talking to you in spirit with regard to the case?' Lisa asked.

'No,' I answered turning away from the wind because my eyes were watering from all the dust that was blowing around. 'I've got the usual parade of people in spirit in my head as always, but no - one who seems to have a direct connection to this case. That might change though once we're in the van and begin the journey.'

Suddenly without warning a torrential downpour of rain began bucketing down.

'Come on guys we're ready!' James called out.

Lisa and I ran over to the van and clambered in.

'Wow!' said James. 'Looks like it's going to be quite a day!' His casual comment would turn out to be an understatement!

As the van headed south on the one and half hour drive to Phillip Island, the conversation was laced with jokes and good humour instead of the usual stilted secrecy. It was agreed before we left the production office that nothing about the Philip Island Case would be discussed until we got there and the cameras were rolling. So for once, without me having to decipher messages from those on the other side to figure out which way we should be going, I could sit back and enjoy the ride. The problem was, I was beginning to feel sick – that nagging, unsettled feeling you get in the pit of your stomach that you try to ignore.

You'll be right, I told myself, always trying to be positive. It's just the wind and the way the van is swaying I told myself logically. Indeed the van was swaying as we cruised at 100 kilometres an hour along the highway into a head wind with the windscreen wipers on double speed to combat the torrential rain. I kept myself right amongst the conversation to keep my mind off of how bad I felt, but a good forty-five minutes into the journey with the van still swaying and the rain beating down so hard that we had to raise our voices; I felt the need to say something.

'Lisa, I'm not feeling very well.'

'I'm not feeling very well either,' she told me. Hearing her say that made me feel better. As a person who never gets car sick, for the first time ever, maybe I was!

Everyone was in on the subject from there on in, and everyone in the van felt queasy. The overall consensus was that we felt that way because of the way the van was swaying in the gale force winds.

'How much further to the island?' Lisa asked.

'Probably another forty minutes,' James said from his seat down the front.

When I heard "forty minutes", the degree to which I felt sick intensified and the safety net of the swaying van hypothesis flew out the window. I knew that I wouldn't last another forty minutes. But rather than refer to that fact I chirped up with … 'Is there somewhere we could stop so that we could have a pee and a drink?'

'Good idea,' said Lisa. 'Put me down for that too!'

Out either side of the van there was just open country, occasional rows of trees on the edge of paddocks as windbreaks, and nothing else. Not even a service station.

'We'll stop at the next place we come across,' James assured us.

Thank god, I thought, because now I was sitting up as straight as possible and breathing slowly to try and encourage the increasingly sick feeling I had to go away. I was praying for a service station, restaurant or shop to appear.

About five minutes later a café appeared and I gave eternal thanks. The café was set back from the road, so we turned off the highway and drove along a dirt road laced with water filled potholes. We found a place to park, and everyone got out of the van. While the rain had eased to a drizzle, the wind hit us immediately. It was bitterly cold! We walked quickly over to the café and went inside where people were sitting at cosy tables enjoying coffee and morning tea. The smell or cinnamon and buns filled the air.

'I'm going to find a toilet,' I told Lisa.

'Do you want a coffee?' she asked.

'Just water thanks.'

Anything to eat?'

'No thanks,' I said. I then had a sudden change of destination as I felt I needed some fresh air! So rather than go to the Men's room, I went outside, searched for some privacy, and found it amongst a row of twenty or so gumtrees that bordered the fence line of the café property. These trees had been around for a while because they were very tall and had wide trunks, big enough for me to hide behind! I walked to the gum tree at the very end of the row. A galvanized shed with some kind of hoeing machine inside was twenty or so metres away, but no person was over there. That was good.

And I was also out of sight from the cafe so I had privacy. Also good! The only eyes watching me belonged to a cow that was braving the wintry conditions in a paddock on the other side of a barbed wire fence.

'Good morning!' I said to the cow. Even in the direst of circumstances, I hadn't lost my sense of humour.

Now I've heard of people hugging trees before, but what happened over the next ten minutes probably wasn't quite what those people had in mind! I hugged that gum tree, leant on it, and threw up at thirty-second intervals. How am I going to get through today? I asked myself in between it all, while also thinking about my nice warm bed back home. I wondered what others in my position would do. Would the big stars quit here and demand to go back to their hotel? I could understand if they did. But you can't go home I reasoned with myself. You're here to do a save on this episode. You can't let them down. They're relying on you. And the money it costs to shoot TV, the crew, their time, the planning, the whole responsibility of it all added to the massive swirl of information that was twirling in my mind.

I glanced beyond the gum tree and saw that James and Lisa were standing beside the van looking for me. I waved to let them know where I was. When Lisa spotted me she looked relieved, and began walking across long, rich, wet grass towards me. I looked to the cow who was observing me with a uniquely bored and unimpressed gaze.

'I hope your day's better than mine!' I said.

'Are you okay?' Lisa asked me as we walked back to the van.

'I'm better now,' I said. 'I just threw my guts up!'

'What had you eaten?'

'Nothing, just the latte you gave me.'

The colour in Lisa's face drained. 'I knew we shouldn't have given that to you,' she said.

'What do you mean?' I asked.

'Well because your plane was late, your latte had been sitting out for a while and gone cold. I reheated it in the microwave for you because we didn't have time to get a fresh one. I'm so sorry!'

'Would zapping the coffee do that?' I asked.

'Not the coffee, the milk,' Lisa deduced.

'Come on guys James called from the van. We need to get going!'

Lisa and I walked back over to the van. 'Scott hasn't been well,' Lisa told James. 'I think he should sit in the front the rest of the way. The swaying of the van in the wind mightn't be so bad up front.'

'No problem,' said James whose seat I'd be taking. 'I'll sit in the psychic hot seat up the back and see what I pick up.'

'Hopefully it's not gastro!' I smiled.

I was left alone for the remainder of the drive to Phillip Island so I could relax and get my thoughts together. A half hour or so later as we passed a sign alerting that Phillip Island was only fourteen kilometres away, the colour was returning to my face.

The Phillip Island Case was from 1986 when 23-year-old Beth Bernard went to work at a farm owned by local landowner, Fergus Cameron. Beth was in her element because she loved animals. It's claimed that Fergus Cameron and Beth were having an affair, and that Fergus's wife Vivienne, was jealous.

Elizabeth 'Beth' Barnard

On the night Beth died Fergus Cameron visited her to see how she was because she had a cold. Police believe that Fergus left Beth alive and well at 9.00 pm. At around 3.00 am a neighbour heard a vehicle drive up to Beth's house. It's believed this vehicle was driven by the assailant, who attacked Beth so ferociously, that a knife hit her straight in her face and knocked a tooth out. Beth's hands were cut as she grabbed for the knife, her throat was cut, and there were other stab wounds and knife injuries to her body, including the letter A that had been carved in her chest, some believe the intended meaning being "Adulteress".

The knife used in the attack on Beth was not cleaned and was left at the crime scene. In addition to that, blood was smeared over Beth's body. Police read this as a sign that there was some deliberate intent to harm Beth, that it just wasn't an event of sudden rage. The perpetrator lingered in the house and had a cigarette, perhaps contemplating what they were going to do next. It was believed the entry point and exit point was the back door, which was left ajar.

At 9.25 am the following morning, police received a phone call saying that there was a possible murder scene at Beth's house. Soon after an officer went inside and found Beth's body in her bedroom. Police believed Fergus Cameron's wife Vivienne had a definite *motive and found her Land Cruiser parked near the San Remo Bridge early the next morning. The San Remo bridge connects Phillip Island to the mainland. It was believed Vivienne had jumped off the bridge.*

Vivienne Cameron

Fergus Cameron was amongst suspects extensively questioned at the time, and police cleared him of any involvement regarding Beth's death or Vivienne's suicide and disappearance. At a colonial enquiry held twelve months later, the coroner found that Beth died from knife wounds to her chest and throat and that Vivienne Cameron inflicted these wounds. Even though Vivienne's body had never been found the coroner was satisfied that she was dead after committing suicide by throwing herself off the San Remo Bridge

I had my own theory about what had happened, and how. By going to the island and visiting various locations, I'd see what energy I picked up, and how that energy matched my theory. If it didn't match, I'd rethink my theory. We crested a hill and the San Remo Bridge came into view.

San Remo Bridge

The water under the bridge was murky grey in colour and very rough, with lots of white foam on waves that were whipped up by the frenzied wind! We crossed the bridge and found a place to park just off the main road. Again, having been handed the case notes, there was no guessing today. I was told the facts.

'This is where Vivienne's car was found the morning after Beth's murder,' Lisa told me.

'Okay, I said. 'Let's get out and see what I feel.'

The side door of the van was opened and an artic chill blew in. The crew and I had brought thick jackets and we certainly needed them! If it were a fraction stronger, the wind would have blown us all backwards. I tried not to be too distracted by how frozen my nose and ears were. Standing where Vivienne's car had been found, I had a clear view of the San Remo Bridge which was only two or three hundred metres away. It started to lightly rain.

The crew followed me down to the water's edge beside the bridge.

'I'm sorry,' I said, 'but I absolutely have no sense that Vivienne jumped off this bridge! None! Her car being left here was a red herring to throw people off the scent. Somebody put her car here to make people believe she jumped. She didn't!'

The wind was aggressively strong at this location at the base of the bridge, and the rain became so heavy that we had to stop filming and runback to the van.

Back inside the van I decided to do some numerology on Vivienne and compared how her profile matched up to the date of her supposed suicide. I saw nothing out of the ordinary when I did that. But when I worked out Beth's date of birth, and compared how her date and spiritual cycles matched up to the night she was murdered, I found that they didn't match! The time the coroner ascertained Beth had died, and what her numerology said, were two different things! According to the coroner, Beth died on 23 September 1986. But that date didn't match a particular aspect of Beth's date of birth that I was taking notice of. However the 22nd of September, the day *before* the coroner found she died, *did* match up!

I explained to Lisa what I found.

'Lisa, without getting into too much confusing explanation of how I worked it out, because it's a mixture of numerology and intuition based on the energy I feel on the island, the key to this case is that Beth died *before* midnight! I feel that Beth had an argument with a man, tempers erupted and she died as a result. I feel the letter A carved into Beth and a doona being pulled up to cover part of her face was deliberately done to look a female committed the crime. The cigarette left behind just happening to be being Vivienne Cameron's brand was a deliberate attempt to make Vivienne look guilty. It's an almost humorously obvious clue set up like an episode of *Murder She Wrote*. It's like Beth's murder was staged or set up in some way! I don't believe that Vivienne killed Beth. And the whole Vivienne suicide scenario is just a cover up for Vivienne's murder by the same man who killed Beth. If Vivienne did jump off the bridge and die, the tides are so strong here that she would have been washed back in.

The day after Vivienne's supposed suicide, a police officer checked salt deposits along the bridge looking for the tell-tail scuff marks where the deposits would have
been disrupted if someone had climbed over the guard railed, and jumped. None of the salt deposits had been disturbed.

'Vivienne didn't jump off the bridge, and she didn't kill Beth,' I concluded. 'And the key to this case is not about trying to find the perpetrator. The spiritual energy surrounding this case is telling me that something's been overlooked … something's missing.'

'Couldn't that be said for all unsolved cases?' said Lisa playing devil's advocate. 'If there wasn't something missing, like a key piece of evidence, the cases would be solved!'

'True,' I agreed. 'Maybe I'm not expressing myself in the right way.' I paused as I thought about the best way to say what I felt. 'Okay, let me put it to you this way. There's a missing key to this case that you *can* find! And you'll find that missing key and have the secret ingredient to solving this case if you do one thing and one thing only … pursue my belief that Beth died before midnight.'

'Can you give a clue as to what that missing key might be?' Lisa asked.

'Sorry Lisa,' I shrugged, 'but I have no idea. Even though I'm psychic I can humbly say that I don't know everything. Anyway,' I smiled. 'It'll give the private investigators something to do.'

My belief that Beth died before midnight led private investigators to trawl through every minute detail of the case searching for proof ... and they found it! In a crime scene photograph taken inside a house on the island, blood on papers can be seen. That blood is Beth's. The pathologist who tested the blood confirms that fact and the results are contained in his official reports which reveal that someone on the island saw the blood and the papers *five hours* before Beth was supposed to be dead!

Amongst almost eighty items in evidence with blood on them, this particular photo of evidence was simply listed as Item 23. Private Investigators had to cross reference pages and pages of documents to find out what "Item 23" was and where it came from, and it didn't feature anywhere in police reports. How did Beth's blood get on those papers five hours before the coroner says Beth died?

Neither Beth's doctor nor the post mortem pathologist were able to estimate a time of death, but despite this the coroner found that Beth died at 3.30 am because a neighbour heard a loud vehicle driving up to Beth's house at that time. But Item 23 – the piece of paper with Beth's blood on it - was seen at a house on the island five hours earlier!

Item 23 is the factual and missing key to solving the Phillip Island Case!

Chapter 12

THE HOUSE

With another week off from between filming *Sensing Murder*, Lee's timing was perfect when he phoned and told me that he'd found a few things out regarding the Beaumont Case. As usual, Lee wouldn't tell me anything over the phone, so we arranged to meet at our favourite café that evening. Lee was his usual happy self when he arrived.

'Do you want anything to eat?' Lee asked.

'No I'm fine,' I said, 'but you go ahead.'

'Be right back,' he said.

I noticed something Lee didn't have the folder that he always carried with him.

'Where's your folder?' I asked when he returned to the table. 'I've never seen you without it.'

'It's back at the office. Everything I want to tell you is up here,' Lee said tapping the side of his head. He sat forward and clasped his hands together, resting them on the table. 'Since we last met I've compiled a list of all the stables operating in the Glenelg and surrounding areas back in 1966. There were a lot of them. Our belief is that someone who worked at one of these stables took the children, and my task was to see if I could uncover any information to substantiate that belief. The bottom line is *yes!* With regard to two of the stables, I've found evidence of paedophilia or sexually deviant behaviour. The house the little girl led you to that night is located around the corner from those two stables. Also, around the corner is a church frequented by people who worked at the stable. The priest at the church at the time is a known paedophile. I've spoken to a couple of men, now in their forties, who were sexually assaulted when they were kids by some of these paedophiles. One of these men is still so traumatised that he could barely speak to me. I just mentioned one of the men's names to him and he started shaking.'

'And Alfred?' I asked.

Lee took a deep breath. 'I can't directly link him to these people, but he did move in their social circles!'

'What about the man in the identikit sketch?'

'Well, the day after the children disappeared a man matching the identikit description was definitely seen at the old section of the Kingston Caravan Park. While that part of the caravan park isn't there anymore, the main building that served as an office is. A man matching the description of the identikit was either staying at the caravan park, or visiting someone who was staying there. In 1966 it was quite an isolated area. There were very few houses there and quite a lot of deviant behaviour went on in the sandhills along the beaches there. The records of who stayed there of course are long gone, but a handful of Beaumont friends now in their late seventies and early eighties did see him at the caravan park when they were searching for the children.' Lee sighed. 'It may well be that Jim and Nancy Beaumont inadvertently knew the main culprit without them ever knowing about his seedier background. And Jane made friends with this man at barbecues and family functions.'

'And Nancy loves a bet,' I added. 'She always has. And back in those days there were bookies all over Glenelg. Even one of our neighbours who I called Uncle Reg was a bookie who worked out of home like many of them did. I'd go over there with my dad when he put a bet on. You didn't have to go to the TAB.

'The list of adult's Jane made friends with or trusted wouldn't be very long,' said Lee. 'The culprit's on that list. He always has been!'

For Lee to find information that backed up my theory should have made me jump for joy. But my reaction was bittersweet, almost sad, which Lee noticed.

'Are you okay?' he asked.

'Yeah,' I croaked, my voice breaking with a sudden wave of emotion. I composed myself as best I could because I was sitting in the middle of a busy café, but still my eyes welled with tears.'

'They were my friends,' I said softly, ' and I miss them … and uh … I can't bare the thought of what might have happened to them, and I can't begin to imagine what Jim and Nancy have gone through … losing three children … it's beyond imagining. They're not together anymore, Jim and Nancy, but they've stayed good friends, and … even though Nancy met another man she never changed her name. She didn't want the children to come back and not be able to find her.'

We sat silently for at least a minute, and then Lee sat forward and rested his elbows on the table. 'The house that the little girl led you to. Might we go there together … now? Do you have time?'

I nodded. 'Sure.'

'Is the little girl here?' Lee asked a half hour later when we were standing across the road from the house.'

'No.'

'If she were, would I be able to see her?'

'I'd say that if the little girl wanted you to see her that you would.'

'And she looks just like a regular ten-year-old kid?'

I nodded. 'Yep, except for the blue light that surrounds her.'

'Hmm,' Lee said. 'Fascinating stuff. 'He looked to the house. 'And what do you reckon about this place? Anything jump out to you on a psychic level?'

'About the house itself?' No I said. 'I believe what I'm meant to take notice of is the land behind the house. It backs onto property that you've now discovered was once a stable.'

Lee peered at me. 'You think the Beaumont children were brought to that stable don't you, the one that used to be behind this house.'

I nodded. 'Yes I do.'

'And the little girl?'

'She leads the way to make sure that I stay on the right track.'

'Do you feel she's connected to the Beaumont Case?'

'I did think about that early on, that maybe that she was a friend of Jane's who I didn't know, but, the little girl's spiritual energy doesn't match up to the Beaumont Case.'

'Who is she then?' Lee asked.

'Ah, I mused. 'That's the million dollar question, and I'm still none the wiser with regard to that. I feel strongly that I've seen this little girl's case on TV, or read about her somewhere. There's an energy around her that she had quite a lot of media attention at one stage or another.'

'Hmm,' Lee pondered. 'That casts a net over a large spectrum of possibilities through many years. Every time a child goes missing or is murdered there's always media attention, especially, in the short term.'

'And,' I added, 'in recent months I've even started picking up on spirits from New Zealand and other countries. I have to consider the possibility that the little girl isn't from Australia.'

'But why would a foreign spirit be helping you with a local case?' Lee asked.

'Who knows,' I said. 'None of us can fully understand how the spirit world works, and my eyes have really been opened in the past couple of months by some of the things that have happened while I've been filming *Sensing Murder*.'

'It would help if she'd tell you her name,' Lee said.

I chuckled. 'Tell me about it! So, where to from here?'

'I'll check this place out,' Lee said as he motioned towards the house, 'find out if anyone who lived here was connected to the stables.'

Chapter 13

CATHY

'Scott you're going to be cut from the Karmein episode,' Lisa told me. 'One of the reasons is that we can't find the cleaner at the shopping centre who you believe saw the van that Karmein was taken in on the night she went missing. We also can't find the people who you say were out walking their dog when the van drove past. And,' she added, 'the two other psychics who are working on the case, their information doesn't match up with yours, well except for where you said that someone else was driving the van that took Karmein. You all agree on that and where it was parked in proximity to the Chan house.'

'Well Lisa!' I said, 'aside from trying to solve the case, as far as I'm concerned the journey which the psychics take the viewers on is an important ingredient of *Sensing Murder!* So what if we don't all agree on everything. It's a psychic show. Not everything's going to be tied up in a nice neat parcel in seven hours or less! And as for you not being able to find the cleaner, or the people walking their dog, so what! Isn't another part of the show having people recognise themselves, jolt their memories, and have them phone Crimestoppers?!'

'I hear you Scott,' said Lisa, 'and I don't necessarily disagree with you either. But it's not my call. It's the producers' decision, and they prefer not to have two different storylines happening in a case. Look, it's nothing personal - it's just the way the show is structured!'

I didn't try to hide my feelings. 'Well,' I said. 'I think that's very disappointing!'

After the Mersina Case had been shelved, I put that situation down to experience and got on with the job. Now that I'd been cut from the Karmein Case, it was a double blow for me, and I was really half-hearted about working on *Sensing Murder*, period! It had been such an incredible day when we filmed the Karmein Case. Between Eloise Worledge leading me to her house, to actually finding the shopping centre Karmein had shown me in a dream, through to Craig Ewen revealing himself, that had been quite a journey, and had all been caught on camera. The day had taken a lot out of me physically and emotionally, not to mention the usual run of sleepless nights I had that led up to the actual day of filming.

On the flight over to Melbourne to film the next case, I stared blankly out the window of the plane and really didn't feel that all my effort was worth it. I could justify the sleepless nights and the pressure of filming when I knew that my efforts were going towards some good. But to know that I could go through it all just to end up on the cutting room floor had knocked the wind right out of my sails, and during that flight I seriously considered quitting *Sensing Murder*! I still had two or three other cases to do. Did I want to? Not if situations like this were going to keep happening. But then I thought about the reason why I decided to do *Sensing Murder* in the first place. To try and bring closure to the families of the victims, and to help solve the case. I thought about how emotional I'd become when talking about the Beaumont Case with Lee recently. Other people who'd been touched by tragedy felt as I did too. It wasn't a good feeling. So because of all these reasons, as the captain announced the plane had begun its descent into Melbourne, I decided to soldier on with the show. Not everything I did would end up on the cutting room floor, and maybe, just maybe, whatever *does* get included would help!

I also decided to create a new challenge for myself on this next case to help raise my personal psychic awareness even higher. The challenge was for me *not* to be given a date of birth the night before filming like I usually would. I wanted only to work from what I was being shown from the main spirit who was stepping forward. For this case is was Cathy or Carol.

As usual, filming began at 9.00 am.

'The first thing I'm picking up on,' I began, 'is a song by Petula Clark called Downtown. Now being a DJ from way back I have a pretty good memory for songs, and I'd say that 'Downtown' was released in 1965. So either the murder was committed in 1965, or the victim was born in 1965. As far as the Cathy and Carol question goes, I'd have to say that we can disregard Carol and go with Cathy. I also have the name Margaret. As a matter of fact, I have two Margaret's. One of the Margaret's is a person connected to this case, and other Margaret is a place like a building or a street. And this is going to sound strange but I also see a unicorn's head. I'm also seeing a lake. with what looks like high cliff walls to one side. It's in a confined space and not an overly big lake. I'm also being shown a building with either three or four arches,' I said as I drew what I was seeing on a sheet of paper.

'I'd say Cathy was about fourteen or fifteen years old when she died.'

'And the possible year she was born again?' Lisa asked.

'1965.'

'Take a look at this card,' Lisa said handing it to me.

I took the card from Lisa and turned it over. The birth date of the victim was 1965.

With the relevant details of the case still to be given to me, James decided they had enough initial information from me, and that we should hit the road. So the crew and I went downstairs, took our usual places in the van, and today's mystery journey began. James turned to face me from his position in the front passenger seat.

'Scott, just to let you know what's happening. We have two or three places that we want to take you to today, and as we only have a certain amount of time to get all this done, we're going to take you to these locations rather than have you try and find them.'

'Fine by me,' I said.

'Good,' James nodded.

As we drove southeast from Melbourne I gazed out the window but nothing in particular took my interest. No sign, no car, no landscape. No building with a unicorn, Margaret, or lake.

Another half hour later and we were driving down the main street of a picturesque suburb. I began to feel increased spiritual energy from Cathy, and I scanned the signs above shops and businesses to see if any were emblazoned with, or incorporated a name or symbol that stood out to me. I was also looking for a building that featured arches similar to the ones that I'd drawn in my sketch. With the energy around the sketch and the name Margaret very strong along this street, one or the other had to be around here somewhere!

With all of us wanting to stretch our legs we pulled over into a parking area in the main street. Outside the van in the sunshine I took in the energy of the hustle and bustle of this place. I wandered a few metres away from the van and came across a sign that said St. Margaret's. Butterflies swirled in my stomach.

'Hey James,' I called out, 'come and have a look at this.'

James walked over to me and the sun caught his eyes as he squinted at the sign. 'Must be a school,' James assumed.

'Or a church,' I suggested. 'Can we go and check it out?'

Don't know if we have time right now,' James told me. 'Give me a sec.' So I stayed out of earshot while he had a discussion with the crew. Finally, James beckoned me over.

'Okay,' James agreed. 'You've got five minutes, ten max.'

'Thanks,' I said.

The cammo filmed me peering up at the St. Margaret's sign, and then followed me as I walked towards some traffic lights and then crossed the road. As I did, a spiritual phenomenon occurred that had never happened to me before. Like a car badly in need of a wheel alignment, I was suddenly pulled to the left! It took all the strength I could muster to keep walking in a straight line. What is causing this I wondered? And then I saw it. I shivered as a jolt of spiritual energy passed through my body. I reached into my back pocket and took out the paper I'd drawn on, comparing my psychic sketch with the architecture of the building. They matched!

I motioned to James and pointed to the building with the arches.

'Here's the sketch, there's the building!' I said happily.

As the cammo filmed the exterior of the building with the arches I felt good that I'd asked we follow the spiritual energy as it flowed rather than come back to it later when the energy might have gone. As a result we'd found a major spiritual clue! Signage indicated that the building used to be the Berwick Post Office.

'What do you think the significance of the Post Office is?' Lisa asked.

'I'm not sure,' I said. 'But I have a feeling that someone who used to work there either knows something about what happened to Cathy, or was connected with Cathy.

'We need to get going,' James told me. 'We'll come back later and check out what St. Margaret's is. But right now we need to be elsewhere!'

Five minutes later we were still in Berwick, but in a residential area next to a highway. James asked me what I felt as I walked up and down a strip of road that ran parallel to the highway.

'I don't really pick up on much as I walk along here,' I answered, 'but I do feel Cathy went that way,' I said, pointing west towards the highway.

'Do you pick up on anything else?' Lisa asked. 'Anything from the houses here?'

The houses were a mixture of brick and what looked like weatherboard and wood, a mishmash of colours and designs, and many looking a little worse for wear.

'I don't pick upon anything else here,' I said.

James decided to cut to the chase, and I was told preliminary details of the Case.

Fifteen-year-old Catherine Hedland had dropped in to her boyfriend's house, the property I was now standing in front of. On a Saturday morning in 1980, Catherine left from here to catch a bus and go to work in Berwick. She never showed for work.

So now I knew that Cathy was Catherine!

We moved on to the next location, and I realised why James hadn't wanted to waste too much time in Berwick. The drive east to Tynong took more than an hour. When we finally arrived on location, it was around 2.30 pm. We turned off the main highway and ventured down another main road surrounded by open countryside, an occasional tree dotting the landscape. But in the distance trees thickly covered the land, which made me wonder how many trees were in this area before it was cleared for farming. We drove into the area where there were more trees, and while the freshness of the area and the sun flickering through the trees was very peaceful, this part of the countryside was eerie.

The van parked on the side of the road and Lisa got out and unlocked a rickety old gate. It opened onto an overgrown, potholed dirt road that meandered for a while, and then disappeared amongst the trees. Through the open gate the van drove, all of us bouncing up and down as the driver negotiated the potholes and bumps of this undulating dirt road. The area was mostly gum trees and natural bushland, thick, untouched, and natural. A minute or so along the dirt road I noticed something sparkling amongst the trees.

'There's water over there!' I exclaimed. 'Is that the lake I was talking about earlier?' The dirt road drifted closer to the edge of the water, and the vegetation became less dense. It didn't look like a lake. 'What is that?' I asked, needing a further clue to the puzzle.

'It's a disused quarry filled with water.' Lisa told me.

'Not quite a lake,' I said. 'But it's another psychic clue we've found that we can tick off.'

We drove on further and the dirt road opened out into a clearing where a vehicle could turn full circle and then return down the way we came. This was as far as we could go, so the van was parked and we got out.

'What is it you want me to look for?' I asked.

'Where Cathy was found,' James answered.

To one side of the van was a smaller track that led into dense bush. I imagined that a long time ago a car would have been able to drive along that track, but it was now so overgrown and covered with tyres and rubbish, that there was barely room for a person to walk along it! Still, there was a difference in energy coming from the track which interested me.

'I'll check that track out later!' I said pointing to it, 'but for now I feel drawn to walk back down the way we came.'

So back along the dirt road I walked to the accompaniment of a variety of bird and bug noises. I wandered over to the edge of the water in the old quarry, surveyed the area, and then turned to face the bushland on the other side of the dirt road.

'Hmm,' I said thoughtfully. 'You're asking me to look for Cathy, but I've got so many people in spirit pulling me every which way that I don't know which way to go first!'

'Who are these people in spirit?' Lisa asked me.

'They're all female,' I explained, and I pointed back down the track towards the gate we'd driven through. 'There's a spirit down there,' I turned from the track and pointed to the dense bush in front of me, 'there's at least two or three over there, and there's another one beyond the van.'

'Why don't we head back towards this side of the van,' James suggested, 'and see what you pick up on.'

So we did.

'James, I'm really sorry I'm so confused,' I said as we walked. 'Would it be possible to do cases in the future where there's only one victim!'

I said that to lighten the moment, but I half meant it too! With me receiving so many confusing energies, it was decided to tell me some additional information.

In December 1980 the bodies of four women, including Catherine Hedland, were found in Tynong North, 74 kilometres southeast of Melbourne, and two others were found in Frankston North in bay side Melbourne. Catherine had left her boyfriend's house to catch a bus to work, but she never arrived at work. A couple of months later police discovered the body of Catherine and also the bodies of Ann-Marie Sargent, (18), and Bertha Miller, (73). When discovered, the bodies had been dead for months, and the victims had been abducted in August and October of 1980. It would take a further two years to find a fourth body through bushland on the other side of Brew Road at Tynong North. The fourth body was that of Narumol Stephenson, a woman abducted from Northcote in November, 1980.

The murders were broken into two groups, the Tynong murders (four bodies found in scrubland) and the Frankston murders (Allison Rooke and Joy Summers were found off Skye Road - the road where Sarah McDiarmid used to live). The women were abducted while waiting for public transport, while walking along the

Street, or while hitchhiking. Police wondered if two serial killers were operating in Melbourne at the same time, or if one man was connected with all the cases!

Several generations of detectives have examined and re-examined the Tynong Case. Some claim they know the identity of the man who killed the women, but that the name was discarded by the original homicide investigators. The suspect was at work at the time of two of the murders and handwritten worksheets were said to prove he wasn't the killer. But the work practices at the factory at the time raise the possibility that either the sheets were falsified, or the suspect could have left his job for hours unnoticed.

The original investigators worked on the belief that an opportunistic killer selected his victims at random. Another line of thought was that Catherine and the other victims were carefully selected by a man they all knew. Catherine and Ann-Marie were dumped naked, while Bertha was fully clothed.

Detectives reinvestigating the Tynong Case also interviewed a notorious serial rapist who claimed to know the identity of the killer.

He alleged the killer was 'Mr Stinky', Raymond Edmunds, who is serving a life sentence for the 1966 murders of Shepparton teenagers Abina Madill and Garry Heywood. The man alleged Edmunds had confessed to a large number of unsolved murders when they had spent many years in jail together. Apparently Edmunds had bragged that his youngest victim was nine. He also alleged that Edmunds knew details of the Tynong killings that were never released publicly.

Police believe Edmunds was responsible for at least 32 rapes and he was the suspect in two unsolved murders before he was arrested in 1985. Detectives tried to interview him over the Tynong Cases in Pentridge in 1992, but he refused to cooperate. Edmunds was familiar with Tynong, and worked and lived on farms in the area. He moved to New South Wales in April 1980, a few months before the four Tynong victims were abducted, and would have had to return to Melbourne regularly to have committed the crimes.

In 2001, Victoria Police told local media they had identified the man believed responsible for six unsolved murders including those at Tynong - but did not publicly identify him. They said that a renewed investigation into the murders had used geographic and criminal profiling and modern analysis to narrow the field of suspects to one, and they were confident they'd identified the person responsible. He had been a suspect since December 1981, and had failed two lie detector tests in relation to the case. The investigation was restarted because new information came to light in relation to the movement of victims after they were last reported missing.

But no charges were laid, and police wouldn't say when they expected to lay charges in relation to the murders or whether they'd re-interview the suspect in the near future.

'Let's focus on finding Catherine,' James told me. ' Where do you think her body was found?'

'I don't know which spiritual energy is which,' I said. 'It's too confusing! I'm now being drawn back down the track past the van.'

'That's not her,' James said.

'Then I don't know,' I said again.

Lisa walked into the bush, and stood by a tree. 'She was found here.' she said, looking to the ground.

When I walked over to where to Lisa was standing, nothing seemed out of place amongst the leaves, rocks and foliage. But the ground did appear to dip lower in the area immediately around the tree. When my eyes locked on that patch of ground, a flood of spiritual information came through to me that I could finally make sense of!

'I feel like Cathy wasn't buried,' I said, 'that she was placed here on top of the ground and covered with leaves and branches. But someone else was left here too. Was there another girl left here with Cathy? But the other girl was buried?' I turned and looked back over my shoulder to the dirt road. 'I can see a dark grey or black car driving along that road. I want to say it's like an old Zephyr or …' I concentrated to try and see the image of the car more clearly. 'It's not your regular type of car. It could have even been partly a sedan, partly a work vehicle, but not a ute. The back of this vehicle was enclosed. It's a more like a European or car, an older model.'

The spiritual floodgate was open now and I spoke as I saw things. 'There was a group of teenagers partying down in that area beyond the van on the night Cathy was brought here. They saw something. There may have also been a fight between a couple of the guys here that night, and one of the guys was taken to a local hospital to get stitches. Whoever brought Cathy here didn't see these young people, but they saw him. The perpetrator had a good knowledge of this area. He probably worked at the quarry over there at the time.' I stopped. 'Actually I think there's more than one perpetrator, that this place was independently chosen by a couple of different men as an isolated place to dump bodies. One of them worked at the quarry and the other

perpetrator had the dark car. When I think of him I think of projectors, and movies. Was there a drive-in around here back in 1980? He could've worked there.'

'Which one of those men do you think killed Cathy?' Lisa asked.

'I feel it was the man in the dark car who likes movies.'

'Do you have a name?' Lisa asked.

I thought about that for a moment. 'No, but I reckon he goes to church and looks like butter wouldn't melt in his mouth. Probably has a wife and kids too. He'd in his late sixties or early seventies now.'

Lisa and I walked to the other side of the van and checked out the area there that had intrigued me so much. On closer inspection I found an incredible amount of rubbish along this smaller track, including a rusted old stove.

'There was definitely five or six young people partying around here on the night Cathy was brought here,' I reiterated. They were here,' I said referring to the very spot where Lisa and I were standing. 'There's also the body of a woman over there that no one's found yet.' I said, pointing deep into the bush

Lisa sighed sympathetically. 'Well unfortunately we can only do one case at a time.'

'Yeah,' I sighed wistfully, 'I know. Just tell that to all the spirits that are talking to me will you!'

It was late afternoon and even though there was still probably half an hour of daylight left, the trees were so high that it was dark down amongst the shadows where we were. So it was decided to head back to Melbourne.

'There's definitely another young woman buried over there on the property to the other side of the road beyond the gate,' I said as we drove back along the dirt road. 'Her energy is really, really strong! And she keeps showing me a big bird. What do they call those birds with the colourful feathers in their tails?' My brain was fried, I couldn't think.

'A Peacock?' Lisa suggested.

'Yeah, it's like a peacock. But a *big* peacock. Don't ask me what it means. I haven't got a clue!'

At the end of the dirt road, Lisa locked the gate and we were on our way.

What the hell is this bird she keeps showing me?' I asked.

'Look in front of you,' James told me as we turned a corner.

And that's when I saw a huge replica bird standing in the entrance to a theme park. It looked about twenty metres high!

The entrance to Gumbuyu Park

'What is that?' I asked. 'Is it a peacock?'

'I think it's a pheasant,' Lisa said. 'Or a lyre bird.'

'Aren't they one and the same?' James asked.

No one was sure. And I didn't care! I was happy just to have the mystery of what the bird was settled!

The drive home was relatively uneventful. It was dark now and getting to Berwick seemed to take forever. As James had promised, we made our way to the street where the sign had indicated St. Margaret's was. The street wasn't that well lit, but as we passed St. Margaret's it looked like it was a school. We parked just near St. Margaret's' main gates.

'I'll only be a few minutes,' I said as I closed the sliding door to the van's side entry behind me. It was a chilly evening as I wandered along the fence line. I reached the school's main gates which were closed, but noticed there was a sign on the gates. Above the actual words was an image that I couldn't quite make out in the darkness. I took a few steps closer and the image became clearer - it was the head of a unicorn!

The St. Margaret School Logo

I stood quietly outside St Margaret's and had a moment. *Every* single spiritual clue that I'd been given, I'd found! In linking it all together I believed that someone who worked at this school, (more so a caretaker than a teacher), and someone who worked at the Berwick Post Office saw Catherine Headland on the day she disappeared. Maybe these people were going to work or shopping, but they both saw the car Catherine got into. That was the connection between St Margaret's and the Berwick Post Office!

I walked back to the van and tapped on the passenger window. James wound the window down. 'You might like to take a look at what I found,' I said.

And so another half hour passed in front of the unicorn as I gave my final thoughts about the case. We filmed using the headlights of the van for lighting.

Still, I wasn't completely satisfied. I'd found one Margaret, but right from the beginning of the day I'd felt there were *two* Margaret's!

Who was the other one?

There was a murder that police believed might be connected to the Tynong Murders. The victim was Margaret Elliott, who was abducted from Box Hill in 1975. The Sensing Murder private investigators also discovered that Margaret Elliot once lived in Berwick just around the corner from Catherine Hedland! They may well have known each other before Margaret moved to Box Hill.

Chapter 14

CRAWFORD

The sound of children laughing and having fun filled the air. Some were on the swings, while others negotiated three different sized slippery dips. Two little girls and a boy were meticulously creating a castle in a sandpit, and there were a number of kids hanging by their hands as they made their way across the monkey bars. There was a roundabout, pony rides, balloons, face painting and the smell of fairy floss ... but where were the adults? Who was supervising this event I wondered? There wasn't one single adult; just a whole lot of kids aged three to twelve!

The little girl in the pink dress ran past squealing as a boy chased her as he tried to squirt her with a water pistol. I recognised the little boy too. It was Craig Ewen, who had first stepped forward to me during the Karmein Case. He and the littler girl were laughing and giggling as she kept changing directions trying to escape getting wet. They didn't have a care in the world!

Was this a spiritual playground? Was this a place where kids on the other side could have fun and enjoy themselves, just like they did when they were alive? Even when kids died, did they still get to be kids? It looked like they did, and I was glad. I looked for my friend Jane. Ah, there she was playing dress-up with Arnna and Grant, something they always liked to do. Jane was dressed like a princess, Arnna was dressed like Tinkerbell the fairy, complete with wings, and Grant was dressed as Superman. My attention was taken away from the Beaumont children when the little girl brought three other children over to meet me. They were the children who'd been playing in the sandpit: the eldest girl looked twelve or thirteen; her sister looked about four, and the boy, seven.

'These are my friends,' the little girl told me.

'Hello,' I said to the three children.

'Hello,' the eldest girl said shyly.

Suddenly these three children became upset as something caught their eye.

'What is it?' I asked.

They ran away screaming, while the little girl in the pink dress his behind my legs. As she did a boy ran past us chasing the three children while waving a large blow-up hammer.

The little girl clung tight to my legs and quivered with fear. 'It's alright sweetheart,' I said. 'There's nothing to be afraid of!'

I was ready to do my next Case on *Sensing Murder*. Production scheduling was so tight on this particular trip it meant there'd be no stay for me in the hotel overnight like there usually would be. I'd just fly in, be met at the airport, do my "thing", and fly out again!

At 10.00 am I wondered through the airport terminal at Tullamarine and down the escalator to the sliding glass exit doors. Lisa was waiting for me just beyond the security doors.

'Ready for action?' Lisa smiled wearily.

'You look like how I feel.' I said. 'Didn't you sleep well last night?'

'Not really,' she said as we made our way outside and across the pedestrian crossing. 'We've been pulling a few all-nighters!'

For each case on *Sensing Murder* a vital part of the show was to have actors recreate the crimes. On the Sarah McDiarmid Case, for example, the film crew and more than thirty actors and extras spent three nights at Kananook station, recreating Sarah getting off from the train and making her way to her car in the car park. There were actors playing everyone from the gang members, witnesses, Sarah's friends, and of course, Sarah. Painstaking efforts went into casting people who were identical in height and look to the real people they were portraying.

Lisa and I dodged oncoming traffic as we crossed a road and waited in a designated pick up area.

'They're doing a circuit,' she told me referring to the crew and the van. 'They should be around again in a sec. Oh, and while we have a moment Scott, you know how with the Sarah Case you said there was a "Ronny" or a "Donny"?'

'Yeah.'

'Well guess what the private investigators found? There's a Ronny *and* a Donny! There's not one or the other, there's *both* of them, and that's what their names are, Ronny and Donny! They were gang members who used to hang around Kananook back when Sarah disappeared.'

I was stunned. 'Wow!' I said. 'I don't know what to say.'

'I couldn't believe it!' Lisa said. 'And it took the private investigators forever to find them. Their names have never been on any public record about the Sarah Case. They're not on the electoral role and because they're crims, they go to a lot of trouble not to be found. But there *was* a Ronny and a Donny who were part of the Jodi Jones gang!'

'Wow!' I said, 'and to think I almost didn't say those names because I assumed at first that the name "Ronald" only referred to one person – the producer's father who died.'

'Lucky for us that you decided to say the name anyway,' Lisa said. 'I also spoke to a policeman who worked on the Sarah Case,' Lisa added. 'He told me that you've changed his mind about psychics because you came up with information that only he and one other officer knew, information that had never been made public.'

'Well,' I said, 'that's another small step in changing police perceptions here on psychics. In America and the UK using psychics isn't such a big deal, but here … ' and I shrugged.

'Is the elderly Ronald still with you?' Lisa asked.

'No. He gradually slipped into the background and disappeared. He's probably watching over his loved ones in the living now.'

'Like a guardian angel?' Lisa asked.

'Something like that. People in spirit watch over us, send us love and positive energy in the hard times to help us get through. It's up to us whether we use that energy, or get all down and depressed.'

Lisa spotted the van approaching. 'Here they come!' she said.

The familiar white van pulled up alongside us. James said hello through the open passenger window. Once Lisa and I took our seats, we were on our way.

'When do you want me to say what I'm looking for?' I asked.

'Let's do that now while we're driving to location,' James told me.

So with everyone in position and the camera rolling, I began.

'First up, I'm looking for a train station,' I said. 'An older style train station with overhead wires. This train station looks different visually and in layout to the way Kananook looks. And at Kananook the car park was more distant from the train station than I'm looking for today. Today I'm looking for a station where the cars are parked at forty-five degree angles by a fence right next to the station building. I'm also looking for a small bridge and a creek. Whoever the perpetrator is, he used to stand on this bridge at the creek and plan what he wanted to do. I also feel that there's more than one victim in this case. There's also a ship, I can't make out the name but it looks like a freighter.'

As we drove along busy roads and through suburbia, there was nothing unusual that stood out to me. And I didn't have anyone on the other side speaking to me or stepping forward either. This was very odd, because the spiritual help I'd usually get didn't seem to be available this time around. All I had was the train station, the creek, bridge, and the ship, and for some reason I kept thinking about the dream I'd had at the playground, in particular the part where the little boy was chasing the three children with a big inflatable hammer. Perhaps those children or a playground was also connected to this case in some way. I was a little concerned that I didn't have more to go on, but I had faith that as the journey proceeded that either further clues would make themselves known to me, or that I'd make sense of the clues I had.

Also, I'd only had a brief look during the audition process, but I was pretty sure that the three children in my dream were the three children in the grainy black and white photo I'd been shown, the photo that had reminded me of the Beaumont children.

The traffic ahead slowed down and stopped as the boom gates lowered at a train crossing.

'Are there wires above that train crossing?' I asked. I couldn't quite see from where I was sitting.

'Yes there are,' James told me from his better view down the front of the van.

'Then there'll be a train station just around here!' I said. 'That'll be the train station I'm looking for.

Sure enough, there was a train station just ahead to our left with cars parked at angles to the station just as I'd described. We kept driving and about five minutes later we turned into and parked in a long suburban street.

'Let's go for a walk,' James said. We all got out the van and prepared for action. 'Which way do you want to go?' James asked me.

'That way,' I pointed to what I assumed was north. With the crew trailing me I slowly made my way along the street to see what I sensed. Suddenly I began to think about a spiritual clue that had first made itself known to me while we'd been filming the Sarah Case. It was the three numbers 186. They were back again, coming through loud and clear! I hadn't thought about them for so long I'd basically forgotten about them. I stopped walking.

Am I looking for house number 186?' I asked. No one replied. I sighed, and continued to walk in the direction I'd been going. 'Thanks for the help … *not!*' I muttered sarcastically. Then I thought oops. I shouldn't have said that because the radio mike that was tucked into my shirt picked up everything, and the soundie would have heard me. I didn't look back to see if he had. I knew that he did!

I looked up and down the street and couldn't shake the thought of 186. Going by the house numbers along here, 186 would be further ahead. Gee this was a long street! We walked further and I slowed down, stopping at least a block short of where 186 would be.

'Do you feel anything here? Scott Lisa asked.

'Yeah, I do,' I answered, 'but I'm still drawn to keep walking to 186 and sort that out first; see if the reason why I'm picking up on that number again on this case becomes any clearer.'

There was a hushed conversation between James and Lisa after which James walked past me.

'Follow me,' he said, and so I did, diagonally crossing the road and standing in front of an ordinary looking house that had a for sale sign. Amongst other things the sign said that the house was "unique for all the right reasons", and that a "blissful family life" could be found there. 'This is the house!' James told me. He didn't elaborate further.

On the wall by the front door I could see there was a three-digit house number. The leaves of a tall potted tree partly covered the bottom part of the first two numbers. I could make out the first number was a 1, and the last number was fully visible and a 6. The curved middle number was the hardest to decipher because the leaves of the potted tree covered it the most. But that number was either an 8 or a 6.

'Is that 1-8-6?' I asked James.

'It's 1-3-6,' he said.

'Well there you go!' I said. '186 and 136. Two different cases, and two very similar numbers! There really are clues to every case in every case!'

'Yes,' Lisa agreed. 'Each case seems to overlap one of the other cases. We've been noticing that for a while.'

'Is that a phenomenon attributed to the type of work we're doing?' James asked, 'or is it just "coincidence"?'

'It's no coincidence,' I said. 'It's been happening too often for it to be just a coincidence!'

'Guys, start walking back to the van!' Lisa said with a sense of urgency. Her sudden urgent tone took me by surprise. 'Let's go! Quickly!'

We hastily began walking back towards the van. As we did I looked over my shoulder to see what all the fuss was about and saw a car driven by an elderly European man drive his car into and park in the 136 driveway. There was a woman I assumed to be his wife in the passenger seat. The man got out of the car and quickly walked after us, shouting angrily!

'Just ignore him and keep walking!' Lisa told us.

'Didn't we get council permission to film in the street?' the cammo asked nervously.

'Yes we did,' said Lisa. 'It's not about that. He owns 136 and isn't happy about us filming his house. As you saw by the sign that's out the front it's on the market, and he's scared that we'll scare prospective buyers off.'

Our hasty pace outdid the man's and he gradually gave up the chase. He yelled a couple of final comments at us in Greek or Italian (I wasn't sure which), and then he headed back towards 136.

We reached the van and a couple of comical asides were made because we must have looked a sight, all of us racing up the street with one old man chasing us. Someone commented that it probably looked like a skit out of the old *Benny Hill Show.*

I brought myself back into the headspace of tuning into the case.

Lisa handed me a black and white photo of a very happy looking man, probably aged in his late thirties. She then handed me another photo of the same man, but it had been altered to show what he might look like now, after which I was told the man's name and all the details of his murderous spree!

Elmer Crawford

Elmer Crawford was born in Canada, raised in Northern Ireland, and immigrated to Australia in 1951 when he was 22-years-old. On 1 July 1 1970, it's believed Crawford murdered his pregnant wife Theresa and his three children in their suburban Melbourne home in Glenroy, house number 136.

Crawford hit Theresa over the head with a thick piece of lead-filled rubber hose while she was sitting in a lounge chair, presumably watching television. He dragged her across the lounge room to the main bedroom and lifted her onto their double bed.

Crawford was an electrician, and had made some devices, each comprising a length of cable with two alligator clips on one end and a three-pin electrical plug on the other. One alligator clip was attached to Theresa's right earlobe, and the other was attached to the fleshy area between the thumb and index finger of her right hand. Crawford then plugged the other end of the device into the power socket and switched it on. The electrified clips left ugly burn marks on Theresa's hand and ear, and it burnt welts into her neck. Normally, the resistance of such a current would blow the fuses, but Crawford had replaced two fuses in the meter box, swapping the thin fuse wire with a strand of normal electrical cable. This ensured the power stayed on as he killed his wife and unborn child.

Crawford then went to the bedroom where his two young daughters slept. Crawford hit eldest daughter Katherine on the head with a hammer, blood spraying over the bedroom walls. He then smashed the hammer against Katherine's forehead, and the hammer became so imbedded in his twelve-year-old daughter's skull, that he had to wrench it out. Crawford then attached his crude, homemade device to Katherine's hand and earlobe and electrocuted her as well. He then hit his six-year-old daughter Karen on the head with the hammer, but for some reason Crawford didn't electrocute her.

Eight-year-old James was found dead in his parents' bedroom. He'd been hit on the side of his head with the hammer and his blood was splattered across his parent's bed. James was also electrocuted.

Katherine, James, and Karen Crawford

Leaving a trail of blood, Crawford dragged the bodies of his family down the hallway, through the kitchen and laundry, and outside into the garage. Crawford placed the bodies inside the family car in a space where the back seat normally was. He'd removed the back seat earlier and leant it against a wall of the garage. He covered his dead family with a tarpaulin and then loaded several plastic containers into the car with them. Also inside the car was a cardboard box filled with old bankbooks, family photographs, an assortment of personal papers, and the homemade electrical leads and hammer that Crawford had just murdered his family with. It's assumed that a small motor scooter was in the boot of the car so he could later return to Melbourne.

Neighbours saw the Crawford family car leave home around 9.00 pm on what was a bitterly cold and stormy winter's night.

Crawford house

Crawford then drove for two and a half hours to Port Campbell and Loch Arg Gorge which is very rugged coastline west of Melbourne. Crawford lined the family car up to plunge over a cliff face into the rough seas, and he'd wired the car so that petrol containers he'd put inside with the bodies would explode on impact when it hit the rocks below. He also made it look like a murder-suicide by attaching a length of hose to the exhaust pipe, and running the hose diagonally across the roof of the car and in through the driver's window. Crawford secured the car's steering wheel so that the car would travel forwards in a straight direction without a driver. He then took out his scooter from the boot and pushed the car towards the cliff edge. The car gained momentum as it headed down a gradual slope and disappeared over the cliff. This is where Crawford's plans went awry. The car didn't explode and fall into the ocean as planned; instead it crashed onto the rocks intact and *upright, and was precariously balancing on a small ledge of limestone 45 metres below which prevented the car from falling into the ocean where it would never be found.*

As the Crawford car was found, still with the bodies inside

It's believed Elmer Crawford left the scene on his small scooter and headed back to Melbourne where he made some cursory attempts to clean the house. A few hours later a school friend of Katherine's knocked on the front door of the Crawford house the next morning to walk with Katherine to school. Crawford is said to have opened the door and told the girl that Katherine was sick with a toothache and wouldn't be going to school that day. There are conflicting reports as to whether this actually happened. Later that morning at Loch Ard Gorge, a group of tourists were walking along the cliff tops when they saw the smashed up Crawford car down on the ledge below.

Police abseiled down the cliff to make the gruesome discovery of who was in the car. A coronial inquest was held in 1971, and Elmer Crawford was found responsible for the deaths of his family. Despite numerous reported sightings in the decades since, he has never been caught.

'Here's the main thing we want to know,' Lisa said to me as we stood on the footpath next to the van. 'Where is Crawford?'

'He left the country,' I said. It was the strongest and *only* feeling I had!

'Okay,' said Lisa. 'But how about this train of thought. Crawford was a miser! He had money and other valuables stashed in the roof of his house. It was also believed that he had money stashed elsewhere too! Would he really have left the country without all that?'

'Look,' I said, 'Crawford may have been a miser, but he left the country! If you think that Crawford's been living the high life up on the Gold Coast for the last 35 years, your mistaken!'

I never got to check out the 186 house further up the street, and never found out whether I was being drawn to that house because of the Crawford Case. Instead, back in the van with time running out to film that day, we drove to a neighbouring suburb where I believed the creek might be that Crawford used to visit. I could visualise him standing on a bridge at this creek, and also walking alongside it when he was planning the murders.

'Did Crawford commit the murders on his own or with someone's help?' Lisa asked me as we drove along.

'On his own,' I answered. 'Although I think he had help to escape.'

Up and down a few more suburban streets we drove, when suddenly a completely different energy stepped forward.

'Guys, I know this is going to sound really strange,' I said, 'and I know we're done with it, but I'm picking up on Mersina Halvagis really strong around here!'

Lisa knew the Mersina Case inside out and upside down, so if there was anything around here pertaining to Mersina, I assumed she'd know about it.

'I don't know of anything around here that could be connected to the Mersina Case,' Lisa said.

James turned around from his position in the front passenger seat. 'I can tell you what you're picking up on Scott! See those trees in front of us,' he said pointing straight ahead. 'Those trees border this side of the Fawkner Cemetery,' James explained. 'On the day we filmed there we entered the cemetery from the opposite side to here. And the grave where Mersina was found is just beyond those trees.'

'I didn't know that,' said Lisa. 'I've never approached the cemetery from this direction before.'

Something occurred to me. 'The day we filmed the Mersina Case I wandered over to a creek that ran through Fawkner Cemetery. That creek wouldn't happen to be the same one that we're looking for today by any chance? In other words, does the creek that runs through the Fawkner Cemetery also run through the suburbs around here somewhere?'

Lisa checked the street directory. 'Yes it does,' she confirmed. 'It's called Merri Creek.'

A couple of left and right turns later and there was the creek meandering through a nature strip of grass and trees.

'There's a pedestrian bridge somewhere along here too,' I said, and then I saw it about a hundred metres ahead!

We parked and I walked over to the bridge and soaked in the spiritual energy.

'Can you feel Crawford around here Scott?' Lisa asked.

'I can feel his energy Crawford around here but it's very weak because it's been such a long time since he was here.'

'Can you actually "see" him?'

'I can't actually see him, but I can feel him. He used to come and stand on that bridge over there, and also walk along the creek and think things over. I also believe that he had help to put his plan into action – help from a man either named Westminster, or that the name Westminster I connected to the case. I believe that after Crawford pushed the car off the cliff that he returned to the house, packed up a few things, and left as quickly as he could. A man by the name of Westminster helped him escape. Part of Crawford's escape involved the train station at Glenroy. There has to be a reason why I picked up on the train station. It can't just be there in the psychic mix for the hell of it. I believe Crawford was smuggled out of Australia on a freight ship and headed to the United States or Canada and then on to Ireland.'

'So you don't believe that Elmer Crawford is in Australia?'

'No I don't. Could he have been connected to the IRA at the time? Did his cause mean more to him than the lives of his family? It's almost like he was "activated".'

'The police did consider the IRA theory,' Lisa told me, 'but discarded it. What about the theory that he went to ground here in Australia?'

'I just don't buy that Lisa. I'm assuming Crawford had a thick Irish accent, yes?' Lisa nodded. 'Well how does someone with a thick Irish accent who murdered his family hide undetected in Australia without being seen by anyone for all these years?!! If the police put out a massive appeal for every person in Australia to keep an eye out for any man in

Australia that has a thick Irish accent who matches Crawford description, there'd have to be someone who'd come forward! Does he never get sick? Does he never file a tax return? Somewhere, somehow, if he were still here, someone would have seen him, or know him. No one's found him because he's not here!'

My belief that Elmer Crawford was no longer in Australia became my spiritual anchor and I set out to prove my point. My first port of call was to speak at length to a close friend of mine, Eliza, who fled Ireland with her family in 1970 when she was a small child, and knew firsthand the problems inherent there. She told me that the worst killers were members of the Ulster Liberation Movement. They killed men, women and children without thinking, blew up cars and burnt down houses. They were later known as the Ulster Volunteer Force.

'Families in Ireland have been killed by their fathers, husbands, uncles and brothers because they knew too much,' Eliza told me. 'Lovers and their families had been killed because one is a Catholic and the other is a Protestant. And if you were seen talking to someone who was marked for death you could also be killed simply by association … not necessarily because you knew anything you shouldn't, but just in case you did! Family members have been known to kill family members if one didn't believe in "the cause" like the other one did. People were shot, stabbed and bashed with clubs and hammers.'

It was Crawford's grandmother, not his mother, who raised him. Crawford's "brothers" were actually his uncles (his mother's siblings). Eliza told me that situations like this were common in Ireland when a Catholic had an affair with a Protestant which was pretty much deemed sleeping with the enemy, so Crawford would have been persecuted as a child as a result. Eliza has seen the persecution - she described it as "torment", and she believed that Crawford would have learned how to hate at a young age, and by what went on around him had the knowledge on how to kill him family the way he did.

The British used electrocution / alligator clip torture against IRA troops in 1970-72. This caused widespread anger and the ranks of the IRA swelled as a result. In retaliation the IRA did the same against British troops, usually attaching one part of the alligator clip to the soldier's genitals and the other part to his hand or ear, and then plugged it into the electricity. Some victims were then shot to make sure they were dead, and then their bodies were dumped.

Between August 1969 and January 1970, communal violence and the ranks of the Provisional IRA swell dramatically. Arms, money and manpower flooded in. Irish who had migrated overseas returned to swell the ranks. Many of these "troops" came back into Ireland through Guatemala in South America and Boston Massachusetts in the US where there is a significant Irish population. They were issued with fake passports and ID's - as killers for the IRA they were never to be traced, or if caught, their true identity never be known. The most common way to smuggle these "troops" into Ireland was by a ship captained and serviced by crew sympathetic to the IRA.

On 30 January 1972, there was huge violence in Ireland, referred to as "Bloody Sunday".

As part of my research into the Crawford Case I also spoke to a postie who delivers the mail on a small CC motorbike He told me that the thought of someone riding such a scooter like that hundreds of kilometres on such stormy night was hard to fathom. Taking into account the strength of the gale force winds that were blowing that night, the postie told me that Crawford would have been exhausted after thirty to fifty kilometres because a person gets the "wobbles" when riding in such conditions. And the scooter would probably have run out of petrol. So either Crawford either carried extra fuel for the scooter, was a superman against the elements, or he had help!

'You've come up with some interesting stuff,' Lisa told me when I presented what I'd found. 'Unfortunately though the other two psychics working on the Crawford Case believe he's still in Australia.'

My footage fell to the cutting room floor again, and I wasn't included in the next and final case to be filmed which was about two nurses in Queensland who'd been hitchhiking and were found murdered.

I went into the Australian version of *Sensing Murder* with high hopes and a sincere desire to help the families of the victims. I also wanted to raise the bar and set an example of what could be achieved on a psychic level, and I did that. To actually lead the film crew to various locations, to come up with specific facts about the cases, and to name people who had never been on public record who actually existed, was a huge achievement, and I was proud of that. But the pressure and process of doing the show had created a number of stumbling blocks, and there had been some disappointing production decisions made along the way which kept knocking the wind out of my sails. And even though the private investigators had checked all the information out first before offering to pass it onto police, it didn't make any difference.

'The police aren't interested,' Lisa told me sadly. 'It's doubtful that anything will happen with the information you and the other psychics have come up with.'

And that's where my journey filming Australia's version of *Sensing Murder* came to an unceremonious end!

Chapter 15

MAYBE

Lee and I sat at our regular table at the café.

'What did you find with regard to the mystery house at Glenelg?' I asked.

'Well,' Lee said as he leant forward and spoke in a whispered tone. 'The house the little girl led you to *didn't* exist in 1966 when the Beaumont children disappeared! It was vacant land, *but*, it was vacant land owned by people connected to the stables, and they used to walk their horses on the property. With this and the other information that's checked out, your stable theory really does have some merit. The children could well have been taken to that property,' Lee said.

'Yeah,' I said, and what if they're still there?'

Lee met my gaze on that possibility, and then sat back in his chair and folded his arms across his chest once again. 'So what do you want to do with this information?' he asked.

'Well,' I said. 'Considering the negative attitude that psychic's get from the police, I'm not sure. I mean if I thought that I could just walk through the doors of the police station and be taken seriously, I would. Because I knew the Beaumont children personally, because they were my friends, maybe this entire journey has been about bringing some form of closure to myself!' I remember a couple of years after the children disappeared I visited Jim and Nancy, and when I walked in to their place there were three pairs of shoes lined up at the back door – Jane, Arnna's and Grant's, just waiting for them to come home. I've never forgotten that, and from that day in particular I made a promise that I'd do everything possible to try and solve the case!'

'What about Jim and Nancy?' Lee asked. 'Would you tell them what we've discovered?'

I shook my head. 'I don't think it's my place to do that. If the police investigated what we've found, felt there was some merit to it, and then decided to tell them, then fine.'

'Well,' Lee said. 'Five years of working on the Beaumont Case! There's not a lot more we can do.' He strummed his fingers on the table. 'I think we've gathered more than enough information to interest the police, but, whether we've done this to purely satisfy our own curiosities, or whether you go to the police with this information, I'll leave it up to you.'

'Do you know anyone at the police department we could give the information to?' I asked.

'Sure I could call in a favour,' Lee said, 'but then there's still no guarantee it would get to the right department.'

'Which is?'

'I'd assume it's Major Crime. And whether I call in a favour, or you contact the police yourself, the word psychic is going to be attached to the information in some manner or form, and the usual reaction to that is negative. The information could end up filed in the trash before anyone reads it or takes it seriously.'

'Hmm,' I pondered. 'Maybe I'll have to wait twenty years or so for a new breed of police officers to come through the ranks who are more open to the spiritual side of things.'

'I think those type of police exist now, 'Lee said, 'perhaps not in great numbers, but they're there. The only problem is that a lot of so-called psychics with no real ability have bombarded the police with their deluded nonsensical thoughts in the past ... '

'Which has stuffed things up for the rest of us,' I said, finishing Lee's sentence for him.

'Well it hasn't helped the negative attitude towards psychics that already existed, put it that way,' Lee concluded.

'Maybe I can change that perception,' I said.

'Maybe you can,' Lee smiled.

I sighed thoughtfully. 'I'll sit on the Beaumont information for now. Whatever I'm meant to do with it will present itself to me when the time's right. I firmly believe that!'

Chapter 16

CLAREMONT

Six months later.

The Drill Sergeant got right in my face, the brim of his hat touching my forehead.

'Are you ready to give your best soldier?' he yelled at me.

'Sir, yes Sir!' I responded loudly.

'Then move!' he yelled.

'Sir, yes Sir! And with that I ran towards four lines of soldiers who were doing push ups on the parade ground. I dropped to the ground and joined in the count with the other soldiers ... 'six, seven, eight, nine, ten!' As I did the pushups, the little girl walked in amongst the lines of soldiers and came over to me. 'What are you doing here?' I asked her as I continued with my pushups. 'You shouldn't be here, I'll get into trouble!'

The little girl pointed towards the barracks.

'Campbell,' she said.

'Yeah,' I said. 'It's Campbell Barracks. What about it?'

I woke up to the sound of birds chirping, my bedroom in semi-darkness. It was 5.56 am. I turned over in bed and placed the pillow over my ears to try and block out the increasingly loud noises of birds chirping their harmonious welcome to a new day. I definitely needed some more sleep!

I was running along a tree-lined road. The sun was shining, the skies were blue, and I felt exhilarated. I had energy to spare!

'Let's sprint!' ordered the Drill Sergeant, who was running beside me.

So we sprinted, trying to outrace each other as our running shoes pounded the pavement. Our sprint ended at an intersection, and the Drill Sergeant paced backwards and forwards as he regained his breath.

'Same again tomorrow?' he asked.

'Absolutely!' I said.

'We'll start from here though,' he added. 'Just for a change.'

'Yes Sir,' I said, 'but where is "here", because I have no idea?'

The Drill Sergeant took out at a pad and pen from his running shorts. 'I'll give you my mobile number,' he said.

As he wrote the number I looked to a car that was parked just in front of where we were standing. The little girl was standing on the footpath next to the car. Inside the car on the passenger side was a woman. Her back was turned to me, but she had brunette hair.

'That's Sarah Spiers,' I said to the Drill Sergeant.

Sarah Spiers had disappeared in 1996 and was believed to be the first victim of Western Australia's so-called Claremont Serial Killer.

The Drill Sergeant didn't react when I said Sarah's name.

'Here's my mobile number,' he said tearing a page from his notebook and handing the piece of paper to me. I read what he'd written. There was no phone number. Instead he'd written a name: Campbell.

I woke up for the second time this particular morning. It was now 6.33 am. The birds were chirping louder than when I'd woken before, my bedroom was full of daylight, and my eyes were stinging from lack of sleep. I lay on my back staring at the ceiling, and sighed. The little girl was sure determined to tell me something about Sarah Spiers. And in some ways, I wasn't surprised because Sarah had been on my mind since my seminar in Perth a couple of weeks earlier where the audience had asked numerous questions about my thoughts regarding the Claremont Case. I'd been touched by how deeply the case had affected these regular, everyday people, and ten years down the track with suspects but no conviction, the Claremont Case was still imbedded in their psyche. These people were desperate for new leads, answers or closure.

'Would you speak to Sarah father?' I was asked.

'No,' I answered. 'I really don't think that's necessary or productive.'

'Other psychics have,' I was told.

'Yes, about a hundred of them from what I hear, and most of them have led him on a merry dance to a point where he's sick of the sight of them!'

'Wouldn't you pick up on more energy about Sarah if you met him though?' someone asked.

'Not at all,' I said. 'My experience is that I pick up enough information without actual contact with the victim's family or friends.'

I couldn't back to sleep so I got dressed and went for a walk. It was just after 7.00 am when I left my house, unusually early for me to be up, and I walked down to a main road a few blocks away. I ran across the road when there was a break in the traffic, and went down a quiet suburban street. The smell of bacon and eggs wafted across the cool morning breeze, as did the noise of a baby crying. I was flying to Perth the next day to check out the Claremont area for myself. Then I'd fly on to Karratha, a two hour flight up the coast, and spend a few days with friends. It was a long commute that I did quite regularly.

I thought back over the two dreams I'd had with the military theme. The name Campbell was interesting. That name had also featured in the Crawford Case. Port Campbell was where Crawford had driven the family car before he pushed it over a cliff. Ah yes, I thought for the umpteenth time. Synchronicity and clues to every case really were in *every* case!

As I walked a four-wheel-drive pulled into the kerb three houses ahead of me. The driver turned off the engine and walked quickly from the vehicle. He looked like he'd forgotten something. Complete with boots, belt and stripes on his lapel, the man was wearing a green camouflage style army uniform!

Out of all the streets and all the directions I could have walked this morning, I'd chosen to walk this way. And out of all the people I could have seen, the first pedestrian I encountered was in the army! Another example of spiritual synchronicity at its best! Whether I was awake or sleep, when spirit wanted me to show me something, or make me take notice of something, they just keep right on showing me!

The rain was bucketing down and the humidity was high as I stood in line at the taxi rank outside Perth Airport, my one piece of luggage beside me.

'How ya' goin' mate?' the cabbie happily greeted me as he bounded out of his taxi. He spoke with an Australian accent, but he was of European heritage.'

'G'day,' I said.

'Just this?' he asked, as he lifted my luggage and placed it in the boot of his taxi.

'Yep, that's it. Rain's pretty heavy,' I said as we got in the taxi.

'Just as well,' the driver replied. 'We're long overdue for some decent rain here. We've had water restrictions for so long I thought I'd have to flush the toilet with Jack Daniel's!'

Good, I thought. He's friendly, he speaks English, and he's got a sense of humour. I've struck the jackpot with this guy!

'So, where to?' He asked as we drove away from Perth Airport terminal.

'The city,' I said, 'but there's somewhere else I'd like to go first.'

'And where's that?' asked the cabbie.

'Claremont.'

My single word answer was enough to make him look at me with a mixture of quizzical suspicion, so I decided to explain myself further.

'I'm writing a book that's partly about the Claremont Case,' I told him. 'and although I've been to Western Australia a few times, I've never specifically been to Claremont. So I wanted to check it out for myself, you know, have a look around, check out the place.'

'No problem mate! Is there anywhere in particular in Claremont that you'd like to go?'

'Not really,' I said. 'Wherever you feel might be of interest to me. Although I understand that some of the girls went missing after visiting a couple of popular pubs there. Is that right?'

'Yeah, Club Bayview and The Continental, although The Continental has gone through a couple of name changes since and is called The Claremont now.'

'How about you drop me off outside The Claremont then and I'll have a look around,' I said.

'No prob,' the cabbie said, 'but you might get a bit wet!' he added as he put his windscreen wipers onto double speed. The airport lights turned green and we veered left and cut across the flow of traffic to the on ramp of the freeway which leads the way towards Perth city centre.

'Is Claremont a beachside suburb?' I asked.

'No. It's about four k's from the beach on the Swan River,' the cabbie told me. 'So what's your book going to be called?' he asked.

'I'm not sure yet.'

'Have you written any others?'

'Yeah a couple.'

'Anything I'd know?'

'That depends. Do you read much?'

'Yeah I like to read. Autobiographies mostly. I like to be inspired.'

'Well, I write spiritual books.'

'Called what?'

'One of them's called *Caught Between Two Worlds.*'

'Sorry. I haven't read it.' The driver peered at me. 'You look familiar though. Have you been on TV?'

'Yeah, a show called *Sensing Murder.*'

'I knew I'd seen you somewhere before,' he said hitting the steering wheel excitedly. 'Your that psychic guy!'

I nodded. 'Yep.'

'Oh man,' he enthused. 'You scared the crap out of me when you went to the train station and reckoned that girl was buried in the dump! Did the police ever do anything about that?'

'No.'

'That's a shame!' he said. 'They oughta take a lot more notice of people like you. And the girl at the train station. Her name was Sarah wasn't it?'

'Yep.'

'I remember that,' explained the cabbie, 'because one of the girls who disappeared from here was called Sarah as well.'

Around 2.00 am on 27 January 1996, 18-year-old Sarah Spiers left her friends at Club Bayview nightclub. She was last seen at a nearby telephone box where Sarah called for a taxi at 2.06 am, but when the taxi arrived the driver couldn't find her. Sarah was carrying her driver's licence and an ATM card. The card hasn't been used since her disappearance, and Sarah is believed to be the first victim of the Claremont Serial Killer.

Sarah Spiers

Shortly after midnight on 9 June 1996, 23-year-old Jane Rimmer disappeared after leaving The Continental Hotel in Claremont. On 3 August 1996, her body was found lightly covered with foliage at Wellard, 40 kilometres south of Claremont.

Jane Rimmer

Around midnight on 15 March 1997, Ciara Glennon left The Continental Hotel in Claremont to catch a taxi home. Ciara was 27-years-old, and was last seen alive outside the Taste of Thai restaurant on Stirling Highway around 12.20 am.

Ciara Glennon

Ciara didn't return home that night and missed a hairdresser's appointment the next day. Ciara had recently returned to Perth from an overseas trip to attend her sister's wedding. On 3 April 1997, Ciara's body was found in bush land more than 50 kilometres from Claremont. Ciara was found partly clothed and had been partially covered with foliage. Ciara had been there for some time and was identified by dental records.

A task force was formed within 36 hours of the second victim, Jane Rimmer, going missing. The task force spearheaded what would go on to be Australia's longest and most expensive search for a killer. In addition to investigating the deaths of Sarah, Jane and Ciara, the task force looked at several other attacks on women in the Claremont area preceding the disappearance of Sarah Spiers.

In the early hours of New Years Day 1994, a man dragged a woman from her car near the Claremont subway after she left Club Bayview. He tried to rape her but she fought him off. Three months earlier, a 31-year-old woman got into taxi near the same nightclub. A man who had been crouching in the back seat tried to overpower her. She broke an ankle after jumping from the taxi.

In February 1995, a 17-year-old girl was tied up with electrical flex, raped, and left for dead at a cemetery after she was abducted while walking home from the Club Bayview nightclub.

'What's the latest on possible suspects?' I asked the cabbie.

'The latest?' the driver queried. 'Nothin' mate. A dead bloody end! Back a few years they had a guy under surveillance for quite awhile … Leon … that wasn't his real name, that's just what the papers called him. Anyway, the police really believed this Leon was their guy. They kept him under so much surveillance and disrupted his life so much that he went to the papers and said that if the police believed he was the Claremont killer that they should arrest him or leave him alone. But they didn't arrest him. Didn't have enough to go on with I suppose. Didn't have that one missing bit of proof. But from what I've heard from cops I've given rides to is that they still think this Leon is the guy who did it. And the murders *did* stop once he was put under surveillance!'

In April 1998 Leon was stopped while driving in Claremont in the early hours of the morning. He was taken to police headquarters, his car was impounded for forensic tests, and police took all his clothes from a wardrobe in his Cottesloe house. Detectives obtained special permission to visit his work premises where they looked over his files, books and computer. He was described as a public servant in his early forties.

In August 1998 Leon failed a lie detector test, which is inadmissible in Western Australian courts. In January 1999 Leon's flat was raided for forensic samples, which were sent to FBI headquarters at Quantico in the USA.

'Aside from Leon, what about other suspects?' I asked.

'Yeah there was also a lot of attention placed on a taxi driver and a friend of his. The Police reckoned those two worked together and picked up girls in the taxi and killed them.'

'And what happened with those two suspects?' I asked.

'Nothin'. And they complained about how stressed they were because of all the pressure the police were giving them.'

In November 2004 an independent panel of major crime experts began a four-week review of the investigation into the disappearance of Sarah Spiers, Jane Rimmer and Ciara Glennon. The panel had access to more than 120,000 pieces of evidence gathered from more than 10,000 interviews.

In February 2006 police announced that Bradley Murdoch (the man convicted of killing British backpacker Peter Falconio) had come under scrutiny as a possible suspect in the Claremont Case. To date, no one has been arrested or charged.

Through the rain and darkness, the lights and skyline of Perth became visible in the distance.

'So. Tell me about Claremont,' I said. 'I'm not familiar with the area.'

'Well, it's a wealthy suburb. Actually it's the suburb that everyone wants to live in!'

'Why?'

'Cause if you can't afford Peppermint Grove, you go to Claremont.'

'What's Peppermint Grove?'

'That's just next door to Claremont along the Swan River where your Bond's and your very rich and powerful live. A lot of people call it Millionaire's Row. You wouldn't get a place there for under three million dollars. And if you can't buy there, your next choice would be to downsize and go to Claremont.'

'So because Claremont is a wealthy area I take it that the pubs and clubs there attract ... how would I say it best ... a higher class of clientele. You know, the places to be, and be seen!'

'Yeah,' said the driver. 'If you're in your twenties, drive a sports car and want to hang around with the young elite, they're the places to go in Claremont. But if you're a bogan driving a crappy car you probably wouldn't be let in.'

We made our way down William Street and over the Horseshoe Bridge which crosses Perth train station. Our conversation lulled for a couple of minutes as we drove through the city. I couldn't make out the Swan River clearly in the rain. Then to my right was Perth's famous Kings Park. I imagined the trees and bushland there reaching up to the heavens and embracing the torrential downpour.

Once through the city the taxi headed west along Mounts Bay Road. We passed a rug centre offering 80% off everything! Didn't they always?

'It's a funny thing,' the cabbie said, but going back about twenty years, so we're talking 1985, 1986 when I was eighteen or nineteen, I used to live in a suburb near Claremont called Nedlands. Back in those days like the rest of the people living there, I was a student going to UWA, that's the University of Western Australia. We'll actually be coming up to the Uni in a sec,' he said pointing to the left of the taxi. 'Anyway, back then the streets in Claremont were really badly lit and I always had a creepy feeling when I walked through there. It was hard to get a taxi around Claremont back then and public transport has always been bad, so even as a bloke, if I'd been out on the town and was on my own, I was always careful about where I went or what I did around Nedlands and Claremont. I wasn't the only one who thought that

way either. There was just something about Claremont and Nedlands that gave everyone the creeps!

'Why was it so creepy?' I asked.

'Wouldn't know how to put it into words mate,' the cabbie told me. 'Maybe back then I was giving you a run for your money and showing off a few of my psychic powers,' he grinned. 'Maybe I smoked so much dope that my brain was fried and I was hallucinating!' He grinned. 'Probably why I flunked out of Uni and ended up drivin' cabs. Whatever … I just knew! People know stuff yeah, get feelings … right?'

'Right.'

'Well I got those feelings in here (he tapped his chest) that there was something creepy about Claremont. Behind the wealth and the homes and the fancy cars was something …' and he thought about the best descriptive word.

'Creepy?' I suggested, borrowing the word he'd used before.

The cabbie shook his head. 'No. Sinister!'

'Where was the place to go in Claremont twenty years ago?' I asked.

'Steve's,' said the cabbie. 'It was a really popular pub for Uni students. But that wasn't in Claremont. That was next door in Nedlands. There wasn't really anywhere to go in Claremont back then that I can think of. And even back then there was no way that we'd let women walk to their cars alone!'

The cabbie waited just down the road with the meter running, reading his newspaper while I had a look around. At nighttime, visitors to Claremont often find themselves on dimly lit Railway Road that hugs the city's main rail link from Perth to Fremantle. Behind lines of stately Cypress trees is the city's historic Karrakatta Cemetery, the final resting place for many thousands of Western Australians. Monuments and headstones bear many famous names including those of university founders, writers and historians, state premiers and other auspicious individuals. Within a few minutes, the bustling nightlife of Claremont seems to rise from nowhere. The now newly named Claremont Hotel, but once notoriously named Continental Hotel, is an impressive two storey Federation style building, and one of the first landmarks to appear. It was once covered in twinkling fairy lights which hid its more darker side, and despite various makeovers and name changes, its reputation as a possible killer's hangout has been impossible to shake.

With the raining easing to a drizzle, I stood outside the Claremont Hotel getting a psychic feel for not only the hotel, but also this entire area. While Ciara Glennon had been the last reported victim, there was the also the spiritual energy of two or three other girls who had gone missing from around here after her. Perhaps these girls weren't noticed by the media or reported missing by their families because they lived a solo life, slipping through the cracks of society. Maybe they were prostitutes or druggies. Perhaps these other girls were from nearby Fremantle, because I kept picking up the name of that suburb. But overall, the word which continued to come in loud and clear was the one I'd seen in my dreams ... Campbell.

'Is there a suburb called Campbell anywhere around here?' I asked the cabbie when I got back into the taxi.

'No.'

'Is there a Campbell Street? I asked. 'Street, Road, Lane or Crescent?'

'Not that I know of,' said the cabbie.

'Can you check the street directory?' I asked.

'Sure thing,' he said, and the cabbie took out his street directory, flicked through the pages, and checked for Campbell.

'There's nothing "Campbell" in Perth at all,' he said.

'Nothing? There has to be!' And I spelt the name for him. 'C-a-m-p-b-e-l-l'.

'Oh "PB"!' said the cabbie realising his mistake. He grimaced. 'I was spelling it without the "P". I should have stayed at University a bit longer!' He scanned down the list of street names. 'No,' he said on this second inspection. 'There's no Campbell around here. The closest Campbell anything is a Campbell Street in Subiaco. That would be the closet to Claremont.'

'How far is that from here?' I asked.

'About seven kilometres northeast.'

I didn't get any psychic feeling from the Subiaco Campbell. 'No,' I said. 'That's not it. So there's no Campbell in Nedlands, Claremont or Peppermint Grove?'

'No.'

'Is there a Campbell Building or anyone of note by the name of Campbell who lives in Claremont?'

The cabbie shook his head. 'No.'

My thoughts went to the Drill Sergeant in the two dreams I'd had, and how I'd seen Sarah Spiers sitting in the Drill Sergeant's car.

'Is there an army base or some kind of military training ground within a close proximity to Claremont?' I asked.

'Yeah there is,' said the cabbie. 'There's a couple actually. There's the Irwin Barracks at Karrakatta, and then there's a much bigger base where the SAS train at Swanbourne, which is about six k's west of here.' All the colour suddenly drained from the cabbie's face. 'Oh my God,' he gasped, 'of course there is. Why didn't I think of it?'

'What?' I asked.

'The headquarters of the SAS is called Campbell Barracks!'

'Let's check it out,' I said.

Of course the best we could do at this time of night was to drive past Campbell Barracks and along surrounding streets, but that was more than enough for me to narrow down my psychic impressions.

The following afternoon I fell asleep on the flight to Karratha and woke up when the First Officer announced we were descending. I looked out the window to a view below of a landscape that never appeared to change in colour with the passing of the months or the seasons. If anything, the Pilbara had become even more barren than when I'd seen it on previous journeys. Undulating hills covered a foreboding world below. Creeks and rivers long overdue to be filled with water, looked like black varicose veins reaching up into the hills and down into the valleys in search of that precious drop. There'd been two cyclones through here in recent times, but the dumping rains they brought didn't appear to have made any difference to the world below.

The coast appeared to the right of the plane and the airport to the left. The plane rocked and dropped a few times on approaching as it hit pockets of hot northerly winds. It had been twenty-nine degrees in Perth. As the plane touched down, the Captain informed us that the temperature here was forty-six degrees.

I picked up my rental car at the airport, checked in to my hotel in Karratha, and then drove eighteen kilometres to the neighbouring town of Dampier. Along the way, to the left of the road, two huge train engines used every part of their combined strengths to slowly pull multiple carriages filled with iron ore across the flat open, rusty brown coloured land. The trains were two and a half to three kilometres long depending on the load, and five or six trains a day (just like the one) travelled the well-worn line every single day of the year!

I looked ahead as the road stretched in a straight line towards the hills that preceded Dampier, and I pictured the place amongst those hills that I'd visit tonight after I'd seen my friends. It was a quiet and spiritual place that I'd discovered on previous visits. It was a place where I could tune into the ancient energies of this timeless land and put my psychic thoughts together. I could relax in the barren isolation of the Pilbara, far away from the troubles of the world, and have some thinking space!

In the early hours of the morning I turned off the Dampier to Karratha road and went to my special place. In everyday life I'd often wonder where other people's special places were, or even if they had a special place in nature where they could go inward and focus on themselves and their spirit. Instead, more and more people have become addicted to communicating *outwards!* Text messaging, mobile phones, the Internet, chat rooms and all the other whiz-bang new fads are welcome and useful technologies. But being the insecure human race that we are, we've turned much of our attention to these outward communications, when the *real* key to life and spirit is to communicate *inwards!*

That's how you become more psychic. Talk to yourself, negotiate with yourself, and be secure in your own space and with your own company. Through the many seminars and thousands of readings I'd done over the years, it was my sad conclusion that most people did everything they could to avoid, delay, or ignore those simple steps. Instead of enjoying our own company, technology has become our constant companion. As far as technology goes, I love technology as much as the next person, but I would no sooner talk on the phone during an aerobics class, fall in love in a chat room, or sit at lunch for an hour texting, than fly to the moon! Sure I love to talk to people, but the greatest communication I have is with myself! That's what I tried to teach others, and I'd keep chipping away, trying to make a difference where I could.

A shooting star streaked across the darkness of the Pilbara night sky. I listened to the quiet for a few minutes. There wasn't a sound to be heard. Not a neighbour, a noisy party, a screeching tyre, or a barking dog. There were also none of the sounds that you usually associate with a night in the bush, like crickets or frogs. But then. This wasn't the bush. This was the desert!

From my vantage point in the hills around Dampier. I had a clear view of Karratha, a sparkling oasis of lights in the distance, and I put my thoughts on the Claremont Case in order.

Firstly, I felt that a gang of four to five people were preying on young women not only in Claremont, but elsewhere around Perth too. I felt that while a man led the gang, one of its members was a woman. Because of some kind of dysfunctional love, this woman would do anything that was asked of her so that she'd gain her partner's affection or approval. All these people were capable of being violent on their own, or in a premeditated pack.

The energy of these people goes back to the late 1980's or early 1990's. They've known each other for a while, and would now be in their thirties and forties. A couple of the gang members will not have proper alibis when Sarah, Ciara or Jane went missing. One of the gang is a taxi driver; he and the other people are, or were mostly likely based in and around Fremantle. One of them lived not too far from where a body was found in that area. These people have laid low while police investigations continued, and since then they've been preying on lesser-known people such as drug addicts and prostitutes. Other women like these have gone missing since Sarah, Ciara and Jane.

Secondly, there is the energy (separate to the gang) of at least three other men who preyed on the women in the Claremont area, working individually without knowledge of the identity of each other. There is a strong sense that all these persons have come under police notice or scrutiny, and continue to be. With so many energies and people involved, a better angle from a psychic perspective is to focus on where is the still missing, Sarah Spiers. Finding her could reveal the biggest and most helpful clues to police.

There's a strong military theme attached to her disappearance. While I don't believe that an army or military person took Sarah, I do believe she was initially taken to a location near the Campbell Barracks or the Swanbourne Rifle Range, or that there is a connection to those areas.

A man was near the Campbell Barracks on the night that Sarah disappeared and saw something which he still feels is irrelevant. It's not. The name Milo is associated with that man. There's also a member of the public who plays army games at the Swanbourne Rifle Range who was out and about on the night Sarah disappeared, and saw something. The strongest name associated with Swanbourne is Ed or Eddie.

While Ciara and Jane's bodies were found some distance from there they disappeared, the energy around Sarah suggests that she was initially taken somewhere very close to Claremont and may still be there. When spirits step forward, often they're accompanied by images, smells and noises.

Around Sarah Spiers there's always the sound of gun or rifle fire!

Two years after the original release of *Psychic Detective*, I became involved in the Sarah Spiers case in a major way. You can read what happened in book #5 of the *Caught Between Two World* series, *Grateful*.

Chapter 17

FALCONIO

There wasn't a breath of wind.

There wasn't a noise.

There wasn't a colour.

There was just … dark.

And isolation.

The little girl in the pink dress stood on the bitumen road beside me.

'We shouldn't be standing on the road,' I told her. 'What if a car comes?'

She giggled, seemingly not worried about a car like I was.

'I have a friend,' the little girl said.

I peered into the darkness, but couldn't see anyone.

'Where's your friend?' I asked.

'I'm here,' came the reply.

The little girl giggled again. The voice had come from behind me, so I turned around, and came face-to-face with Peter Falconio!

'I am so pleased to meet you,' I said. shaking Peter's hand.

'Thank you,' he said.

The little girl in the pink dress clutched Peter's legs and giggled again. 'Take me for a ride Uncle Peter,' she said excitedly.

And with that Peter rose from the ground with the little girl clutching his legs, and they dipped and soared across the desert sky. I suddenly found myself hovering in the sky watching them. Although it was dark I could still see how far the flat, arid landscape stretched in every direction. There was just nothing for as far as the eye could see. The three of us returned to the ground, the little girl hugging Peter as they landed.

'Peter,' I said, 'people are looking for you. Can you help me locate where you are?'

'Where the truth is,' Peter replied.

'What does that mean?' I asked.

'There's a lake, a pub and UFO's,' Peter said. 'The letter "W" is important,' he added. 'Look for more than one "W" at the pub where the UFO's. are.' He looked to the little girl who sent him a big smile, and he looked back to me. 'My family and my friends are in pain. Please tell them something.'

I waited to hear what Peter wanted me to tell them, but instead of speaking, he embraced me tightly. The immediate energy I felt from him took my breath away. It was like a lightning bolt of love, energy and peace surged through my body. The rushing energy of unconditional love that I felt from him was incredibly humbling.

'Tell them I love them,' Peter softly said.

Journalist Leigh Reinhold was on the phone asking me to be part of a special "Where is Peter Falconio?" feature in *Woman's Day* magazine. Leigh and I actually went back

A long way. In 1993, Leigh wrote the first story about me to be featured in a national magazine. The story revealed my attempts to warn actor Brandon Lee of the danger surrounding him on a film set. Even though my Hollywood contacts had made sure that my warning did get through to Brandon, his response was: 'If I'm meant to die young like my father Bruce Lee, then so be it'. Two months later Brandon was killed on the set of the movie *The Crow* when a stunt gun misfired during an action scene.

'Scott. I know it's out of the blue, and rather short notice, but do you reckon you could give me just a few lines on where you think Peter Falconio's is?' Leigh asked.

'I don't know, Leigh. Hasn't enough been written about the Falconio Case already?'

'Come on Scott,' Leigh said, brimming with enthusiasm. 'Let me hear what you think! I'm assuming that you do have a few thoughts with regard to Peter.'

'I reckon everyone in Australia would have a theory or two,' I said.

English tourists, Peter Falconio and Joanna Lees were driving along the Stuart Highway in the Northern Territory on the evening of 14 July 2001.

Peter Falconio & Joanna Lees

Having left England eight months earlier, they'd travelled through Asia and arrived in Australia in January 2001. They bought a Kombi van in Sydney, and had travelled to Canberra, Victoria and then on to Ayers Rock and Alice Springs. From Alice Springs they headed north to Ti Tree where they refuelled at sunset.

Not long after dark they were pulled over by a man in a white four-wheel drive ute, a few kilometres north of Barrow Creek, and 300 kilometres north of Alice Springs.

The man parked his vehicle behind them and said there was something wrong with the exhaust of the Kombi van. Peter Falconio got out and walked to the rear of the vehicle to have a look. He has not been seen since. Joanna Lees was forced from the Kombi van at gunpoint. Her wrists and legs were bound and she was also gagged. Joanna Lees struggled with the offender who punched her while he was trying to put her into his ute. The man was momentarily distracted and Joanna managed to escape into nearby bushland, where she hid behind bushes on the far side of the highway. The man searched for her with a torch and his dog. Joanna found her way back to the highway at about 2.00 am and was picked up by a truck driver who took her to Barrow Creek.

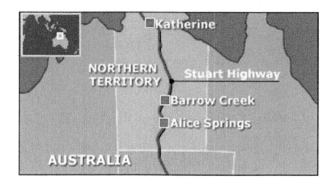

The Kombi van was been found a couple of kilometres north of Barrow Creek. It had been driven off the highway and into bushland. Police set up roadblocks on all major highways in the Northern Territory, and there were several alleged sightings of the man in his vehicle at different locations across the Territory. He was described as Caucasian, and about 40 - 45 years old, His hair was dark, straight, and shoulder length with grey streaks. He had a long thin face, a droopy, grey moustache, was of medium build and had an Australian accent. He was wearing a black baseball cap, with a motif on the front, a long-sleeved dark T-shirt and heavy jeans or canvas-like pants.

Closed circuit television footage recorded at a truck stop in Alice Springs just hours later purportedly showed the man filling up with fuel.

A forensic anatomy expert confirmed that the man on the video footage was Bradley Murdoch. Even Murdoch's father said it looked like his son. In August 2002 Bradley Murdoch was arrested in South Australia and charged with various offences including the alleged rape of a twelve-year-old girl and her mother, for which he was acquitted. During the course of this trial a swab was taken for DNA testing to assist the prosecution team in the Peter Falconio Case.

Just months after this acquittal, the Peter Falconio trial began in Darwin.

During the trial, while Joanna Lees couldn't remember certain parts of what had happened to her on the night of the attack, she was immovable on the fact that Bradley Murdoch was the person who had ambushed her and Peter Falconio

In December 2005, after a nine-week trial, Bradley Murdoch was sentenced to life in Darwin's Berrimah Jail after being found guilty of murdering Peter Falconio and depriving Joanne Lees of her freedom. The jury of six men and six women deliberated for eight hours and rejected Murdoch's denials of innocence.

The Case against Murdoch was considered largely circumstantial, but it was the match of Murdoch's DNA to a smudge of blood on a T-shirt worn at the time by Joanne Lees which was the most telling. Expert evidence stated that the chance of the DNA belonging to Murdoch was 150 quadrillion times more likely than it belonging to anyone else. Murdoch couldn't explain how a smudge of his blood came to be on Joanna Lees' T-shirt.

Although comforted by the verdict, the Falconio family still didn't know what had happened to their beloved son and brother Peter, who was 28 when he disappeared. Peter's brother Paul said, 'The most important thing to my family now is to find Peter's body!'

'Let's get past the theories,' Leigh said. 'I'm talking about thoughts and visualisations; all that psychic stuff that you do! Has Peter Falconio spoken to you, "stepped forward" as you say?'

'Yes he has.'

'What did he say?'

'He told me that the letter W is where the truth is.' I heard Leigh draw breath on the other end of the phone. 'What's the matter?' I asked.

'One of the other psychics I spoke to about the case said the same thing!' There was a pause before Leigh asked, 'What else did he tell you?'

'The other main clues are a lake, a pub, and UFO's. And it's around those three things that the letter W is very strong. Actually, there are two W's, in the name of the location.'

'Hmm,' said Leigh thoughtfully on the other end of the phone. 'Doesn't ring a bell with me. When you say UFO's do you mean that Peter is in an area where there's been UFO sightings, because that's certainly true of some specific areas in the Northern Territory.'

'Well, that could well be,' I said. 'Peter keeps showing me cartoon like drawings of a crescent moon, flying saucers, and Saturn with its rings. He told me that the truth is near the pub where the UFO's are.'

There was another thoughtful hmm from Leigh as she wrote down what I was telling her. 'Anything else?' she asked expectantly.

'Well, there's also the word "Devil". Whether it refers to how Peter feels about the person who killed him, or whether it refers to a place, I don't know.'

'Do you know where Peter's body is precisely?' Leigh asked me.

'There is no body!' I said. 'You're talking remains, not a body. And I feel that his remains are near the two W's.'

'Do you think he was buried?'

'Well,' I said, 'if Peter Falconio had been buried out in the open, his bones or remains most likely would've been found by now because the dingoes, feral pigs, parenti lizards or some other predatory animals would have dug him up. I'm more inclined to think that I he was hidden away out of sight in a ditch or a drain beside a road, where even if his remains were disturbed, you wouldn't notice.'

One of the interesting aspects of psychic detective work is that when I'm on the right track, I always get a confirmation. Two weeks after I spoke to Leigh, a couple of old friends dropped in to see me. Originally from Adelaide, they'd been living in Darwin for a number of years, but had finally decided to come home. Over dinner the conversation turned towards their drive back to Adelaide and how they felt a little edgy when they passed through the location where Peter Falconio and Joanne Lees were ambushed. When I'd told them about my conversation with Leigh Reinhold two weeks earlier, and the psychic clues of the lake, the pub, the UFO's, the two W's, and the word Devil, my friends just about choked on their meal. Having just done the road trip from Darwin, the locations they passed were fresh in their minds, and they were able to shed some light on the matter.

The word Devil related to a rock formation called The Devil's Marbles.

But that wasn't the only psychic clue they solved for me that night. The two W's pointed to a place called Wycliffe Well. Many Northern Territory roadhouses find a gimmick to distinguish themselves from the next fuel stop up the road. Wycliffe Well, on the Stuart Highway 127 kilometres south of Tennant Creek, has a strong UFO theme, with murals, spaceship models and smiling images of alien creatures to greet you at the petrol pumps. And as for Peter Falconio also mentioning a lake in the dream I had, my friends told me that there was a lake out the back of Wycliffe Well.

Owner Lew Farkas in front of Wycliffe Well

I phoned Leigh the following day to pass on the clarifying information.

'Is there any way of including Wycliffe Well in the story as the specific place Peter is referring to?' I asked.

'I wish we could,' Leigh told me, 'but the story has already been printed!'

So while the *Woman's Day* story did mention Wauchope and Central Mount Wedge as possible W locations, it didn't include my belief that Wycliffe Well was really the specific location that Peter was telling me about!

Chapter 18

NEW ZEALAND

About a year after I finished filming the Australian version of Sensing *Murder* I was speaking to Yvonne, a producer from New Zealand. She was sussing out whether I'd be interested in working on their version of the show, and had called me one afternoon from her office in Wellington.

'We saw you on the Sarah episode at Kananook,' Yvonne told me. 'It was just amazing!'

'I didn't know it had screened over there,' I said.

'It hasn't. Not yet anyway. We had a tape sent over to our office here.'

'How many New Zealand episodes are you doing?' I asked.

'We'll be doing six. How did you find working on the Australian version?'

'Mostly good, but it had its ups and downs like anything I guess.'

'Scott, we've tested 70 psychics over here and only came up with three or four people who are of the standard we need for the show. We'd love you to work with us as well!'

After I finished the Australian version of *Sensing Murder*, I'd pretty much decided that I'd never do the show again because of the way its format was structured. Having to work out who the case involved and what happened to them, was a problem. Trying to solve a case in a few hours of a single day was also a problem, as were all the sleepless nights leading up to a case. Trying to sort out the many spirits who were talking in my head leading up to a case was alsoan issue. So was battling through all that and possibly having everything I filmed end up on the cutting room floor.

'What if some of things that I come up with don't match up with what the other psychics think!' I asked.

'Well,' said Yvonne, 'I don't have a problem with that. It's not expected that the psychics will all agree. The only time we wouldn't use anything is if a psychic got a mental blank while filming and just didn't come up with anything, you know, couldn't tune into the case at all. Aside from that, as it *is* a psychic show, once you or any of the other psychics are on the trail of something, I don't think it's in the best interest of the case to cut anyone out just because you don't all agree. As far as I'm concerned, in amongst the most unlikely scenarios could hide the biggest clue to solving a case!'

It was refreshing to hear Yvonne say that. 'Then you and I will get along just fine!' I said.

'Why, were there problems when you filmed before?'

'Yeah, a couple of times, which to be quite honest, put me off doing the show. But I'm really happy with what you've said, because I feel the same way. You have to let the psychics be psychic!'

'Exactly,' Yvonne agreed. 'Does that mean you'll do the show?' Yvonne asked.

'Yes, but on one condition.'

'And what's that?'

'That I only commit to one case to start with. If that works out, then we'll talk again.'

'That does make it a little difficult,' Yvonne told me. 'We were hoping that you'd do more than one.'

'Yeah I figured that,' I said. 'The thing is Yvonne, knowing that I have to do more than one case puts too much pressure on me. Too many dead people start talking to me all at the same time! I mean they probably will again anyway, but I can deal with that better if I'm only committed to doing one case at a time. I'm not trying to be difficult. I'm just letting you know that after my experience filming the show here, it's an issue I need to address.'

Yvonne was quiet on the other end of the phone as she considered my terms.

'Okay,' she finally said. 'Agreed! Now Scott, there's a few things that I need to tell you. The New Zealand version of *Sensing Murder* is run the same way the Australian version is. I can't tell you where in particular in New Zealand it is that you'll be going. All I can tell you is that there are two flights are involved. One to Auckland, and then another flight to somewhere else, and that second location could be on the North or South Island. Also Scott, please don't take this the wrong way, but there's nothing on the Internet about the case you'll be doing. That's why we chose it. Not because we want to test you out, but because it's a lesser known case that's slipped amongst the cracks and deserves a higher level of police attention. Once it's aired, there may well be some stories that pop up on the Internet about it due to renewed interest, but right now, there's nothing.'

'So it's not the Kirsa Jensen Case then,' I said.

Yvonne didn't miss a beat. 'No it's not,' she said.

Kirsa Jensen disappeared in 1983. Her case remains one of New Zealand's most famous unsolved mysteries.

'What made you take an interest in the Kirsa Jensen Case?' Yvonne asked.

'I have friends living in Queensland who are from New Zealand,' I explained. 'They asked me what my thoughts about Kirsa were. I didn't know who she was at the time, but I looked into her case and came up with a few things.'

'Well you must tell me what you feel about Kirsa when you're over here,' Yvonne said. I heard her rustle some papers on the other end of the phone. 'Okay, next we have to figure out when can we get you over here!'

We settled on a date six weeks ahead, and Yvonne told me that my travel itinerary (as far as my journey to Auckland went) would be sent through in due course. When it was, I was immediately concerned! Whoever made the arrangements had only allowed an hour for me to catch a shuttle bus between the Domestic and International Terminals in Sydney, make it through customs and board my flight to Auckland. Being a seasoned traveller I knew that kind of timeframe was basically impossible, and when I emailed Yvonne voicing my concerns, her reply said that the travel agent had spoken to Qantas who in turn had guaranteed that an hour would be enough time. Now call me psychic, but that's where I became jittery! I knew it wouldn't be enough time, and it wasn't.

My flight from Adelaide arrived late, and as I exited the flight and made my way into Sydney Domestic Terminal, a call was going out for me to make my way to the transit lounge opposite Gate 2, *immediately!* Of course because I was running late, Gate 2 was right down the other end of the terminal from where I was, so I had to run, and upon my arrival at the transit desk I was ushered downstairs to the transit bus waiting lounge. While my running to Gate 2 had been great for my cardiovascular fitness, it had been fruitless in other ways because the transit bus didn't leave for another five minutes. By the time I was shuttled across to the International terminal and I made my way up the stairs to customs, my flight to Auckland was scheduled to leave!

Customs was jammed with queues of departing passengers, there was no way I was getting through in a hurry, and my name was being called out over the intercom again, a semi-pleasant but stern request for me to, 'make my way to Gate 20 because my lateness was delaying the scheduled departure of the flight!' I looked for any opportunity there was for me to quicken this process, but there wasn't any. I'd just have to bunker down and wait my turn. I knew this would happen, but rather than get uptight about it, I laughed out loud as I saw the humour in the situation.

'What's funny?' a man standing next to me asked.

'People should take more notice of psychics!' I said.

I thought the flight would leave without me, but it didn't, my delayed boarding causing it to depart almost half an hour late.

On the flight to Auckland, I thought about what I'd achieved on the *Sensing Murder* cases so far, and planned what I wanted to achieve this time. It was all well and good to take the TV audience on the journey of discovering what the case was, and determine who the main players were and who might be guilty of committing the crime, but now that I had a few cases under my belt I felt it was more important to steer away from all that and concentrate on finding the missing key to solving the case. Whether it be an eyewitness, or missing evidence, or something in the investigation that was overlooked, I wanted to find the key that would actually link the perpetrator to the crime and prove their guilt. In the rush of filming the show previously, and with the spirits leading me every which way, I'd never had a chance to really do that before. This time, I hoped I would, and to try and do this was another reason why I agreed to do Sensing Murder in New Zealand.

I arrived in Auckland at 3.30 pm their time. From the International Terminal I made my way over to the Domestic Terminal where I had one more flight to catch which I discovered was to a place called Tauranga on the North Island, but that flight wasn't until 5.30 pm. By now I was feeling worse for wear, and had been travelling for just over seven hours. I found a quiet corner near the departure gates and sat out the two hour wait, nodding off a couple of times. Ten hours after I left Adelaide I finally arrived at Tauranga's regional airport on the North Island just after 6.15 pm. Located in the Bay of Plenty, Tauranga has rolling surf and endless coastline making it one of New Zealand's most popular tourist destinations.

Yvonne met me with a friendly hug. In her early thirties, she was a mum with a recent newborn baby.

'It's been pouring with rain here,' she told me, 'but thankfully it should be fine and sunny for filming!' We drove away from Tauranga airport. 'We're all staying at the same place,' Yvonne continued. 'They're very nice serviced apartments just near Mount Maunganui in the heart of Tauranga. I think you'll be very comfortable there. When do you want me to give you the date of birth for the case?'

'Well,' I said. 'Considering how tired I am not tonight. Best not to encourage any spirits to start talking to me until I get some sleep. Why don't we leave it until tomorrow.'

'Whatever you think,' said Yvonne.

The schedule was that the following day was set-aside for me to rest and recuperate, and then we'd film the day after.

When we arrived at the apartments Yvonne and I chatted for about half an hour, and then with both of us weary, we said goodnight. I'd meet the director and crew tomorrow.

The traffic zoomed past me either way as I stood beside the busy highway. The sun shone in my face. Why did I forget to bring my sunglasses? I could've used them today. A blue/grey coloured car approached from down the highway and slowly drove into the area where I was standing. An Elvis Presley song was playing on the car's stereo. A man was driving, and there was another man in the passenger seat. In their early to mid-thirties they both looked like they'd drunk too much beer and smoked too much dope. They had that worn out tired look that people get when they do everything to excess!

The driver had straggly hair in need of a good cut. The man in the passenger seat wore a beanie. He looked out the open window of the car and spoke to me.

'Do you like our car?' he asked.

Actually, I thought it was a bit of a shit heap, so I answered diplomatically. 'A friend of mine's got one just like it.'

The Elvis song got louder.

'There he is over there!' I heard the driver say.

And with that they sped away, did a U–turn, and parked their car across the highway from me. There was a tug at my hand. I looked down. It was the little girl in the pink dress.

'They're the bad people!' she told me.

I suddenly found myself on the other side of the highway standing behind the car. It slowly drove away and Daniel Morcombe peered out the back window. Recognising his face, I tried to run after the car and yell for help, but my legs were working in slow motion, and my voice was a whisper.

'Daniel!' I tried to yell, but I could barely hear myself.

The little girl ran around me. 'They're getting away. They're getting away!' she told me urgently.

The Elvis song grew louder!

I woke and looked at the bedside clock. 2.03 am. Who the hell is making that god-forsaken noise at this time of the morning? I got out of bed, pulled back the curtains, and looked four floors down to a neighbouring house where most of the lights were on. " I Can't Help Falling In Love", by Elvis

Presley was blaring from a stereo, and a very drunk man was staggering around his driveway singing along (badly) to Elvis at the top of his voice. I sighed as I watched tonight's free entertainment from my balcony window. It was going to be a long night!

I curled up on a lounge chair, picked up the remote control to the TV, and channel surfed, but I wasn't taking any notice of what I was seeing in front of me. I was taking *more* notice of what I was suddenly seeing on a psychic level. It was a photo I'd been shown while working on a previous case; a photo of Elmer Crawford's house with a caravan out the front.

I couldn't shake that image. But, why? Why would I dream about Daniel Morcombe and now 'see' this photo?

'You shouldn't be trying to figure this out now,' I told myself out loud. 'You've got another case to work on first.'

Still, it was hard to shake the images I'd just seen. The man on the passenger side of the car, In the dream I'd seen his face so clearly, and I felt sure he was one of the men involved in Daniel's abduction. I could get the computer programmer to draw an identikit picture for me. Ah, but wait a minute. That particular software was back in Australia in Melbourne, which didn't do me any good here. As for the car in the dream, I'd recognised the make! And as for Daniel … there wasn't any sign of a struggle … no fight. He just sat in the back seat of the car looking over his shoulder out the window to me. Did that mean he willingly got in the car, and then realised his mistake?

'How did you sleep?' Yvonne asked the next day.

'At first, great!' I said, 'but I got woken up by a guy next door who was singing Elvis songs.'

'Is that what that was!' Yvonne said. 'I thought I was imagining things!'

'I smiled. 'Unfortunately it was real!'

'Were you able to get back to sleep?' Yvonne asked.

'Eventually.'

'Well hopefully tonight he won't give you an encore performance,' she said. 'So, what do you want to do now? Would you like to stay here and relax, or would you like to go to lunch?'

'Lunch sounds good!' I said. 'Anywhere that serves great coffee!'

We found a café a couple of streets away in the main street of Tauranga.

'I'll need to give the date of birth for the case,' Yvonne reminded me.

'No problem,' I said. 'When we get back to the apartment you can give it to me then.'

'Will do,' Yvonne said. 'We both sat quietly for a few moments eating our lunch. Yvonne broke the silence. 'So Scott,' she said. 'You told me on the phone that you'd looked into the Kirsa Jensen Case. What are your thoughts?'

On 1 September 1983, 14-year-old Kirsa collected her horse, Commodore, from the paddock next to her home, and rode Commodore to Awatoto Beach in Napier. It's believed Kirsa arrived at the beach at 3.30 pm. She was seen at 4.00pm by a passer-by who noticed a girl being held by at arms length by a man, described as

European, 1.8 metres tall, and around 45 - 50 years old. The passer-by also saw a white ute parked nearby. The ute's flat deck had brown sides.

Another witness stopped and talked to Kirsa, who had blood on her face, which she told him had happened when she fell from her horse. She told the witness that someone had gone to inform her parents and that she expected them to arrive shortly. The witness left Kirsa thinking all was under control.

Another witness said that around 4.30 pm he drove past a white ute that was crossing the bridge. The driver was described as a European male, with brown hair and approximately 20 - 30 years old. He had his arm around a girl passenger's shoulders and was driving using one hand. Several witnesses saw Kirsa's horse Commodore after this, around 4.45pm securely tethered.

At 5.30 pm Kirsa's mother and friends started to look for her. The police were advised of her disappearance at 6.45pm and started a preliminary search. They found
Commodore wandering aimlessly near the Tutaekuri River Bridge. The search continued till around 11.30 pm when it was called off for the night, to be started again at first light.

The following day the search resumed with the help of volunteers from the neighbourhood. Police divers searched the Tutaekuri River and other waterways. Police also appealed for the man Kirsa was seen talking to, the driver of the white ute, to come forward for questioning.

On Tuesday, September 6th, the search was extended and in the days that followed a video retracing Kirsa's movements was shown on television nationwide. Police asked for the public to phone in *registration numbers in their quest to find the man in the white ute with wooden sides.*

Police believed that Kirsa had fallen from her horse and that the man who had been seen with her and said he'd help by contacting her parents, had in fact abducted
her.

The main suspect police were interested was John Russell, who already had a conviction for rape. Russell identified himself as the man who was seen with Kirsa. Police tested over a hundred samples of fibres taken from his home and went over his truck, but no evidence was found. Russell then proclaimed his innocence and believed he was being persecuted. On several occasions Russell admitted to killing Kirsa Jensen, but always recanted, and Police never had enough evidence to take the Case to court.

Russell spoke to Kirsa's parents, telling them that he wasn't involved in their daughter's disappearance.

Shortly after this, Russell was committed to a psychiatric facility. A month
after his release, John Russell hung himself.

'So,' Yvonne said, 'the big question has always been did Russell kill himself because he couldn't live with what he did to Kirsa, or did Russell kill himself purely because he was mentally unstable and suffered some form of delusions?' Yvonne shot me a curious glance and rested her elbows on the table. 'What do you think?' she asked.

'Well,' I began, 'I can't match the energy of Russell's name to Kirsa's energy, and I can't match his admissions of guilt to Kirsa's energy either. I feel that if he were involved, that he would have led police to where she was. I have the name Adam or Adams, not Russell. Kirsa's spiritual profile shows that she was in a particularly strong romantic and emotional cycle in the months leading up to when she disappeared. I believe that while Russell may have been in the area when she disappeared, that Kirsa had actually hoped to cross paths or meet up with a young man that day, a young man aged in his late teens or early twenties. I think she was quite smitten with him. I believe he holds a big part of the key. So does a grain or feed store. I also see a warehouse or barn with hay, horse bridles, bags of oats or wheat … and a cellar.'

'Was Kirsa taken to this place?' Yvonne asked.

'I wouldn't rule it out,' I said. 'Now, Kirsa told a passer-by that she got a bloody nose when she fell off her horse.' Yvonne nodded. 'Well,' there's something not right with that. If Kirsa *had* fallen from Commodore onto her face, then she would have done more damage than just a bloody nose. Even if she'd fallen on the sand at the beach she would have hurt herself and had other lacerations, maybe even a broken nose, a concussion, or other injuries. I'm more inclined to think that she had an argument or a scuffle with someone. I'm inclined to think she was attacked by the guy she was smitten with, and was too embarrassed to admit it to the passer-by who saw her.'

'So,' said Yvonne. 'Let me see if I've got your thought process right. 'You think a guy Kirsa liked forced himself on her, panicked, went back, and made the situation worse, or a guy Kirsa liked saw what happened and was too scared to speak up because he made advances on her and thinks he'll take the rap.'

'Pretty much,' I said. 'The key to finding Kirsa Jensen has always been to find the guy she liked, not by chasing John Russell.'

'It's an interesting theory,' Yvonne said. 'I know that Kirsa's file remains open and that police hope they'll find her remains one day.'

I met the director and crew later that afternoon after which Yvonne gave me

the date of birth relating to the case I was working on.

The following day the camera rolled just after 9.00 am. Once the usual introductory questions were asked, there was something I needed to get off my chest.

'I'm not quite sure how to explain this,' I said, 'but I feel like the person I'm supposed to be tuning into isn't really that person! Like if you told me their name that I'd tell you it *wasn't* their name! I just feel that something's not right, like I'm dealing with two of everything!' I shrugged. 'I don't know how else to explain it.'

'I think I might understand what you're getting at,' said Yvonne, 'But let's just work through this step by step and see what happens, okay?'

I had a sudden thought. 'Is this a case about twins?' I asked.

'No.'

Hmm. This case *wasn't* going to be easy!

'What can you tell me from the date of birth I gave you?' Yvonne asked.

'Well, the energy around this date is definitely female. And here's what I'm seeing in spirit. There are two ladies with the letter L, and they're both standing side by side.' I moved my hands to the right. 'The lady over here is Linda. I don't get the surname totally, but I want to call her Linda G.' I moved my hands to the left. 'The other lady over here has a very exotic, European, old-fashioned name. She's the one who I want to focus on, the one who I feel the case is about.'

'Can you describe the way she looks?' Yvonne asked.

As Yvonne asked that question the exotic lady stepped forward further. 'The best way I can describe her is that when I look at this lady I immediately think of Selma Hyack or the lady that Tom Cruise used to go out with, Penelope Cruise. She's a European, very pretty dark skinned young lady!'

'Age?'

'Mid to late twenties.'

The exotic lady sent me some images and symbols which gave me a better understanding of the kind of person she'd been.

'The overall impression I get of this lady is that she really lived life on the edge and I don't think that she played by all the rules. She was a very nice person and had a good heart, but there was a side of her that was hidden, a side of her that people didn't know about. Maybe that's why I feel that she's two different people!'

Yvonne smiled to me from her position beside the camera.

'Very good,' she said. 'Now, in light of you picking up on the letter L before, I'm going to show you the victim's name.'

Yvonne handed me a card with the name Laverne printed on it. I instantly became confused. I was looking at the name Laverne, but I still felt that I didn't have the correct name!

'This is the weird thing that's been haunting me ever since we started filming today,' I said. 'When you show me this name, I feel like it isn't true, that it's not her name, that it's some kind of trick. I feel that people called her by a different name, perhaps a nickname! It's almost like she's two different people!'

'Try and separate from that confusion regarding the L name,' encouraged Yvonne, 'because you're on the right track. What about a surname? Do you get any feeling on that?

'Yes I do. William, Williams or Williamson.'

Luana Laverne Williams

On 5 June1986, 25-year-old Luana Williams disappeared from her Tauranga home without a trace. Her home was left unlocked and nothing was disturbed. There were embers still glowing in the fireplace, a half a glass of sherry was sitting on the table, and an unsmoked cigarette had burnt down entirely to a butt and ash. Luana had left behind her passport, her purse and her cigarettes. She has not been seen since and her body was never found. Thirteen years after she vanished Luana was officially declared dead. While Police originally treated the Case as a missing person inquiry, there was a dramatic turn of events in 1994 when police began a murder inquiry into Luana's disappearance.

Luana was of European, Cook Island and Cherokee decent. She grew up with five brothers and sisters who called her by her middle name, Laverne. But to her friends she was known as Luana.

On the night of Luana's disappearance her boyfriend came home from the pub at 6.00 pm. Luana had prepared dinner for him while he was out. They had an argument because Luana knew he'd been seeing someone else. After dinner, the boyfriend went back to the pub and stayed there until closing time. At 10.30 pm he left the pub with friends, and went to the house of one of the friends. He returned home in the early hours of the morning and found that Luana wasn't there. It wasn't until later that same morning after he woke up, that he reported Luana as missing.

Luana had a history of working in massage parlours, and her association with known drug dealers landed her in jail. Upon her release Luana wanted a fresh start and worked in a factory and did cleaning jobs to get by. Because of Luana's background, the District Commander at the time told his police officers not to treat her disappearance as a murder/homicide, but instead as a suicide!

In 1994 a new District Commander opened Luana's file and reclassified her Case from a suicide to a murder investigation. Renewed searches with failed to recover Luana's body in likely bushland areas. There were also rumours that Luana's body had been dumped at sea. One thing police all agree on is that Luana knew her killer!

Yvonne checked her watch. 'We need to get on the road soon,' she told me. 'Is there anything else that you want to tell me before we do?'

'Yes. There's a house number 28 that's important. I'll try and find the street where that house is! There's also two males that I'm interested in. There's that double up again!' I said. 'This case is like Noah's Ark. There's two of everything!'

'What do you think happened to Luana?' Yvonne asked.

'Well, it's almost like an argument erupted, or some jealousy happened and she got taken out! That's how I feel at this stage. I may change my mind later. I've also got what I assume is a Maori name trying to come through. It's the first time I've been to New Zealand so I'm not sure of its correct pronunciation. '

'Give it a go,' Yvonne encouraged good-heartedly.

'Well, it's something like Oda ma poo or Oda Mooda something. Does nothing ever happen on Smith Street?' I asked. 'It would be far easier for me if it did!'

Yvonne and the crew appreciated my sense of humour. It lightened what is often a very depressing and subdued atmosphere during filming. We took a minute's break to relax and stretch our legs, and then it was back to my seat where I was handed a skilfully traced blank map of the Tauranga region, and asked to identify where Luana wanted me to go. I pointed to two specific areas that were in close proximity to each other.

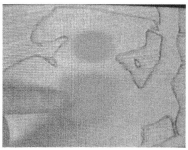

I would later discover that one of the areas I'd Identified was where Luana had grown up. The other area was where she worked. The red dots are a special effect added to the map in postproduction. They were not on the map when I pointed to it. The photo shows a quarter of the total map that I was looking at.

It was a bright sunny Friday, just as the forecast had promised. In a different van, but in the familiar right-hand, back seat, I discovered something spiritually interesting very quickly. Whether I'm in Australia or another country, the degree of difficulty in finding what I'm looking for was just the same. In Melbourne I didn't know which direction I was going in any more than I did in New Zealand. So all I could do was let the spiritual energy lead me. As we drove toward the areas that I'd pointed to on the map, I had another attempt at deciphering the Maori name.

'I'll try and spell it,' I said. 'It's something like O-D-O-M-O-O-T-U or ODOMOOTI.'

'Look over there,' Yvonne said as she pointed to the left hand side of the van.

I looked out the window and saw a street sign. The sign read Otumoetai, which turned out to be the suburb where Luana grew up.

'How do you say that?' I asked.

Yvonne told me the correct pronunciation, and I was relieved to get that difficult name out of the way.

'Now I'm getting a street name that begins with a B,' I said.

For at least ten minutes we drove around without any success in finding a B street that matched the spiritual energy I was feeling Amongst many B streets that we'd driven past were Bridge Street, Brook, Branch, and Beach. Beach had a good vibe to it, but I didn't feel it was quite right. Then I had a psychic flash.

'There isn't a street round here called Birch is there?' I asked.

A quick check of the street directory revealed there *was* a Birch Street close by. It was a narrow, winding, highly industrial street populated with factories, warehouses and small businesses. We slowly drove up and down it two or three times, and I became increasingly frustrated.

'My definite feeling is that Luana worked here and that someone who was in on the crime worked along here too. But I'm not seeing what I want to find. I'm looking for some kind of food factory that makes chocolates, biscuits or chips - snack foods. But I'm not seeing anything like that. I'm just seeing crash repairs and a scrap yard. What I'm looking for may not be here anymore.

The scrap yard was actually the site of the former Mr Chips factory where Luana worked for several years before her disappearance. Yvonne had no idea there was a connection between Luana and Birch Avenue. Such information hadn't come up in their research, but would later.

We gave up trying to find what I was looking for in Birch Avenue, and stopped at a picturesque park to film what other thoughts I had on the case at this stage.

'I'm very much drawn to the name Colin,' I said. He's about 5 ft 11 - 6 feet tall, and has shaggy blonde hair and blue or fair eyes. I feel that Colin worked in the area on Birch Street. She also had a brother, nephew or a sister who worked in Birth Avenue as well.'

Luana did work with a man called Colin when she worked at the Mr Chips Factory. My description of him was accurate. When Luana was in her early twenties she had a relationship with him. Luana also had a sister who worked with her at Mr Chips.

'There was an altercation between Luana and another person in this park where we're standing.' I said. I focused harder on the spiritual information that was coming through so that I could sharpen the images that I was receiving. 'Actually I wouldn't be surprised if someone who worked at the factory knew what happened to Luana. Birch Avenue is like a centre point around which a lot of the information that's needed to crack this case can be found.'

'Was there a vehicle involved that you can identify?' Yvonne asked.

'Yes. There was a white tray top ute that draws trailers around or has bikes in the back, and a smaller red car like a Toyota Corolla or a Datsun Coupe.'

'Can you describe the area where Luana's body is?'

'I feel it's in scrubby bushland, and that it's not too far away from civilisation.'

It was close to 2.00 pm by now and no one had eaten, but we all voted to delay lunch and continue filming while my spiritual meter was running on overdrive. It was decided it was time for me to try and find the street that had the mystery house number 28. I was drawn to streets just a short distance away from Birch Avenue, and we drove up and down the residential streets until finally I was drawn to one particular street!

'The property at number 28 in this street is significant to Luana and whoever took her.' I said. 'A man who lives at that property has information.'

We drove along the street and counted down the house numbers. Oddly enough we reached the end of the street where numbers were in their forties without ever seeing a 28.

'Did we miss 28?' I asked.

'I didn't see it,' Yvonne said.

So we u-turned and slowly cruised back up the street. Yvonne counted down the house numbers out loud as we passed the properties.

'36, 34, it has to be on this side, she said. '32, 30 ... 26!' The van stopped. between 30 and 26.

'Where is 28?' I said. 'Am I having a mad moment and can't see it? Is there a unit or something behind one of these houses?'

No there wasn't. Nor was there a vacant block of land where number 28 could have once stood.

'There is no 28 in this street!' Yvonne said. 'It doesn't exist!'

'But why not?' I asked. 'Why would a seemingly normal suburban street be missing a house number? I told you guys this morning that there's something weird about this case, that there are double ups and two different meanings to everything! First the factory wasn't there and now the 28 house isn't here! This must also mean Luana's body is missing!'

This was indeed the case. I hadn't been told yet that Laverne had gone missing and had never been found.

'Scott, we'll move onto the next location,' Yvonne told me. 'See what you pick up when we get there.'

The nearby location was right next door to a large hardware store. To one side was the store and its car park, and to the other side were houses. I hadn't said anything, but on a spiritual level I was now lost, and felt that I was wasting the crews time. The factory wasn't there, house 28 wasn't there. I wasn't having a lot of luck!

And as for this new location?

'I don't really pick up anything here,' I replied lamely.

So to help me out, Yvonne told me that the vacant block we were standing in front of was where Laverne had lived. The actual house hadn't been demolished; it had been relocated to another part of Tauranga.

'So what we've got,' I said, 'is a factory that isn't there, a house number that isn't there, and Luana's house isn't there! Everything in this case is missing or has been removed!'

'Might be a good time to finally have a late lunch!' Yvonne suggested. She looked at her watch. 'It's almost 3 o'clock!'

So we drove to a nearby café area, and she and the crew had lunch. I didn't eat anything because I didn't feel well, and I politely watched the hungry crew devour everything in sight. But it wasn't a case of me not feeling well and being sick like I had been when working on the Phillip Island Case. I was just physically and emotionally drained from all the dead ends I was coming up against.

When we left the café it was just after 3.45pm, and there wasn't a lot of filming time left. As we walked back to the van, Yvonne told me what was going to happen next.

'There's a place we want to take you to. I can't tell you what this place is, or why we want to take you there. We just want to see if or what you pick up on once we get there.'

'Okay,' I said flatly. It was all I could do to muster a smile and be upbeat.

Twenty minutes later we'd driven away from the hustle and bustle of suburbia, and into the scenic and hilly countryside. The highway entered a more densely vegetated area and this is where the van slowed, turned off the highway, and drove along a road that gently sloped down into a valley.

The change of feeling in me was immediate, a little like stepping out of air-conditioned comfort into a forty-six-degree day. Wherever Yvonne was taking me, or whatever she wanted me to see, I didn't want to go! And I was surprised at how upset I suddenly felt.

'Listen guys,' I said with agitation in my voice. I don't know where you're taking me or what you want me to see, but there's a whole different set of spiritual energy here, and its got nothing to do with the case we're working on. As a matter of fact, it's confusing me, so I'd rather just get out of here!'

My feelings were ignored and the van drove deeper into the lush countryside. We passed water cascading over large rocks, and I grew more agitated.

'Who else got knocked off around here?' I said. 'I've got people left right and centre taking to me! What is this horrible place?!! Can we just leave please!'

But like a determined, impertinent child, the van kept going forward. Images and energy from those on the other side flashed around me like a massive thunderstorm! We travelled another fifty or so metres and in a car park ahead was one solitary red car. It triggered a sudden unsettling image.

'Oh fuck!' I exclaimed. Who was the girl who was found dead in a red car in the car park?'

On 10 January 2005, four months before we filmed the Luana Case, 24-year-old Natasha Hayden was found murdered in her red car at McLaren Falls. I was still to be told that McLaren Falls was the name of our current location. The information concerning Natasha would be told to me by Yvonne a couple of months later, because on the day of filming, she didn't know about Natasha.

This area is awful!' I said, and I put my hand over my face, covering my eyes. Because of my emotional reaction I missed a moment of spiritual synchronicity. A white tray top ute drove past the van. I'd earlier said that a white coloured ute had taken Luana on the night she disappeared.

'Do you pick up anything about Luana in this area?' Yvonne asked me.

'No, 'I answered. 'All I've got is the dead girl in the red car! I don't get any sense of Luana here at all! As soon as we turned down this road it began to happen. Whatever has gone on recently here is quite upsetting to me! Don't film me for a sec mate will you please,' I said to the cammo. He dutifully lowered the camera so that its focus was off my face, although I figured he was still rolling to pick up anything verbal I said.

By now I was a mixture of anger and tears. I am never doing this fucking show again!' I said slowly and sternly. 'Just get me out of here!'

The van did a three-point turn, and we headed back up the road towards where we'd turned off from the highway.

'Why did you bring me to this horrible place?' I asked Yvonne.

'Because one of the other psychics working on the case thought that Luana's body had been buried somewhere around here. It's a national park called McLaren Falls.'

The van continued its journey out of McLaren Falls and I became calmer. I also began to feel a little embarrassed. 'Listen,' I said. 'I'm really sorry that I got so upset.'

'No. No,' Yvonne soothed. 'It shows how human you are, how real what you feel is. We made it to the end of the road that leads into McLaren Falls, turned right, and headed back towards Tauranga. The camera was still lowered.

'Listen,' said Yvonne softly. 'I know you were upset but are you sure that you didn't feel Laverne's energy there at all?'

'No I didn't.'

'What did you feel?'

'Just the energy of the girl in the red car. Hers was the strongest. I have the name, Natasha. And she's showing me a birthday cake, and it's like the cake that she missed out on. I feel it was her birthday and she died on or close to her birthday. It's just so overwhelmingly sad. ' What a beautiful location for such horrific things to happen,' I said.

Yvonne initially felt that what I was picking up on was the fact that Luana disappeared a month before her 26th birthday But when Natasha Hayden's father Brian contacted me after this episode of Sensing Murder aired, he told me that his birthday was soon after Natasha died, and she'd always get him a cake.

On the drive back to Tauranga there wasn't much conversation. It had been a long, emotional day! It was dark as the van arrived back at the apartments.

'I can't wait to have a shower,' I said.

'By all means freshen up,' Yvonne told me. 'But you'll have to put the same clothes you're wearing back on because we haven't finished yet! We need to film a summary of the day and you need to be wearing the same clothes for continuity.' She checked her watch. 'So we'll see you again in half an hour!'

With me showered, and fresh, and back in my grotty clothes, I didn't add much more to what I'd already said at the summary, even after Yvonne revealed the names of who police considered possible suspects in the Luana Case. She also told me that I'd been right about the lady who I'd called Linda G. Linda was having an affair with Luana's boyfriend while he was living with Luana. Linda's surname started with a G, and she later married Luana's partner.

When the camera was turned off and the crew were packing up, Yvonne took me to one side.

'Scott, are you really serious about not doing any more episodes of *Sensing Murder*?'

'Yep. I've had enough. I just don't want to do it anymore!'

There was a short pause as Yvonne thought about what she wanted to say. 'I respect that,' she finally said. 'It's been quite a day! But if you do change your mind, there is one other case that we'd like you to do.'

'I won't change my mind Yvonne,' I said. 'What happened today was the final straw. I've had enough of being under the pressure of trying to solve a case in a day! *Really* had enough!

I was one of three psychics who worked on the Luana Case. The other two psychics believed that Luana was buried at McLaren Falls. Filming on two different days, they independently led the film crew to the exact same area at McLaren Falls which they believed was Luana's burial site. And on those two separate days, they ended up five meters apart in a park that covers 170 hectares! One of the psychics brought a spade and started digging for Luana, to no avail.

Once the Luana episode was screened, police said they wouldn't dig up the McLaren Falls area identified by the two psychics as the burial site of Luana. Police said information must be evidential before it can be used as the basis of further investigation. Inquiry head Detective Sergeant Eddie Lyttle said that no further digging at the falls had been carried out by police since filming, nor would there be. 'We would really need a witness account or something like that because it's incredibly difficult to find someone who's buried,' he said. 'While police would love to go up there and start digging away, spiritual communications were not considered a creditable foundation for investigation, and the nature of the area made it largely impractical!' Mr. Lyttle said McLaren Falls had not previously been identified by police as a potential murder site. He added that buried bodies were notoriously difficult to find, pointing to one Auckland Case where a killer led police to the burial spot and they still could not unearth it. Mr. Lyttle also said that some information passed on from the psychics was not revealed the final edit of Sensing Murder. This included profiles of three people who played important parts in Luana's disappearance. Mr. Lyttle could not divulge details for legal reasons of who those people were. He said police had kept some Case details from Sensing Murder producers.

Former Detective Sergeant John Bermingham was extremely disappointed with the police decision not to further excavate the site but said cost and resources may have played a part. 'It's hard to know what their real reasons are,' he said. 'If they had their own theory then they would but it's because a psychic has said it that they're saying no.' But Detective Sergeant Lyttle said police had legitimate reasons for not excavating. 'Police have had a number of psychics identifying various locations,' he said, 'and we just can't go searching everywhere because we don't have the resources. Mr. Lyttle said he was happy with the public response to the show. By the following morning after it aired, 24 people had phoned police - several of whom provided fresh information relevant to the Case.

Luana's family was disheartened by the police refusal to dig at McLaren Falls. Younger sister Melanie said she sat with her parents and watched Sensing Murder at their Otumoetai home while her mum shed 'gentle, silent tears of relief'. All three had seen the episode before it went to air, but Melanie said each screening opened the door to healing a fraction more. Melanie said her own psychic awareness had made her recognise McLaren Falls' importance soon after Luana disappeared. But the immense stress on her family meant she put all of her energy into supporting them. Melanie also said that she and family members were frustrated that police didn't take psychic's more seriously!

Natasha Hayden's father Brian also told me that the police didn't give much credence to anything I or the other psychics had said. He told me that they were critical of the fact that I'd referred to Natasha as "Natasha" instead of Tash as she was more commonly known.

'You can't make people believe what they won't want to believe!, I told Brian. 'They will always try to find a way to pick a hole in it or discredit it.'

'Well,' told me. 'The interesting thing is that yes, Natasha was "Tash" to her friends and family, but whenever she was being introduced to someone formally or to someone she didn't know, she always referred to herself as Natahsa. In my opinion, introducing herself as Natasha is how I believe she would introduce herself to you from the other side or how you would pick up on her energy.'

That evening after filming, Yvonne and I went out for dinner. I asked to be seated at a table at the front of the restaurant by the windows. I just wasn't in the mood to be seated in the middle of the restaurant and be surrounded by other people and all their different energies.

'Well I'm all for some quiet space too!' Yvonne told me as she pulled her chair in closer to the table to get comfortable. 'So are you recovering from the day?' she asked me.

'I'm fine,' I answered, 'and I'm glad my appetite's returned.'

'Yes, you haven't eaten all day,' Yvonne said. 'Did you feel unwell on any of the other cases that you worked on?'

'Only once,' I told her, 'and that was because I drank a dodgy coffee.'

'So where to for you now?' Yvonne asked me as she unfolded her serviette and placed it on her lap.

'It's straight back into work for me,' I said. 'Lot's of readings. I'm always flat chat. And,' I smiled, 'I have my karate which keeps me focussed and sane. And I have a couple of other projects on the go.'

'Well don't get me wrong,' Yvonne said, 'because what I'm about to say isn't some sneaky way to get you to change your mind; but I'm sorry that you won't be doing any other cases with us.'

'Well I appreciate that,' I said. 'But you've now seen firsthand why working in the pressure cooker of Sensing Murder isn't what I want to do anymore.'

'Does that mean you won't be doing any more psychic detective work at all, ever?' Yvonne asked.

I nodded. 'I'm probably heading that way, yeah. But not before I finish one last case that I've been working on privately.'

Yvonne looked at me with a curious stare. 'Which case is that?' she asked.

Chapter 19

DANIEL

Author's note:

In 2011, forty-one-year-old Brett Cowan was arrested and charged with Daniel Morcombe's murder. I wrote about Daniel in the original 2006 release of Psychic Detective. With information about the case now released by police, I'm able to include some author notes signified by (**) and you'll see where I was right about what I felt and where I was wrong.

Rest in peace Daniel.

Queensland has always been like a second home to me. There was a time when I lived in the Sunshine State for up to three months of the year, so I know the place like the back of my hand.

I'd received hundreds of letters and press clippings about Daniel Morcombe. In particular I remember a large brown manila envelope postmarked from Cairns. It was so full of newspaper articles about Daniel that it was bursting at the seams and had been extensively bound with masking tape to keep it together! Inside the manila envelope were numerous press clippings of all shapes and sizes, with any lines of text that the sender considered important for me to know about highlighted in green marker pen.

Amongst the mass of mail were handwritten letters pleading for me to help find Daniel. There were also a couple of letters calling me a bastard because I hadn't helped! Unfortunately those types of misguided people have no real concept into what a day in the life of Scott Russell Hill really entails - and that it isn't just a matter of me dropping everything and hopping on a plane!

As a psychic detective, for me to seriously look into a case meant I had to find a two-week window in my diary to focus totally and solely on just that case. If I didn't prioritise then the information I received from spirit could quickly became a jumbled mess of clues, because what I received wouldn't just be about the case I wanted the clues to be about.

Think of it like this.

Ever tried listening to forty conversations at once and then try to make sense of it all?

Not easy!

So like a policeman standing in the middle of a busy intersection when the traffic lights are out, I'd learnt how to prioritise; to channel the spiritual traffic in an orderly pattern so that it didn't all crash in the middle! Don't ask me how I do the prioritising because I haven't got a clue. Like so many things I've had to figure out over the years I had no mentor, no real guidance or clues from an outside influence. I just shone my own light into the darkness, tried different things, discovered what worked and didn't work, and found my own way.

Some of the journalists who'd extensively covered the Daniel Morcombe Case are friends of mine, and they'd told me about what some so-called psychics had thoughtlessly told Daniel's parents about his demise without tact or regard for their feelings. I hated hearing about stuff like that. It puts all the work of more thoughtful and considerate psychics back about fifty years!

So because of the negative spin other psychics had put on Daniel's Case, I felt discretion was needed, so I didn't make a big song and dance about me going to Queensland.

Some media outlets had wanted to follow me around if, as they told me, "you visit where he disappeared at some stage". But instead of letting the media know I was "in town", I snuck in unannounced! A group of passengers did recognise me though while I was boarding the flight to Queensland, and they happily told me, "we feel safe to fly on this plane because you wouldn't be on it if it were going to crash!"

Funny!

As I tune into people through their dates of birth, I re-checked Daniel's date and spiritual profile out thoroughly on the flight to Queensland. From the first time I'd looked at his date through to this visit, everything I felt, all my thoughts and impressions regarding what might have happened to him remained the same.

Would I change my mind on these thoughts and psychic impressions? Experience had taught me that I probably wouldn't. But that was the purpose of this journey; for me to not tune in from a distance, but to tune in starting from where Daniel was last seen and have fresh perspective.

I'd also noticed there were many aspects of Daniel's spiritual profile and Jane Beaumont's which were exactly the same! While Jane was a Virgo and Daniel a Sagittarius, there were exact similarities between their attitudes, reactions and behaviour. So having known Jane, it gave me some extra insight into Daniel.

Although I was familiar with the Sunshine Coast, I hadn't specifically been to the Kiel Mountain overpass before, so rather than hiring a car and finding it myself, I chose to take a taxi from Caloundra where I was staying and let the cabbie drive me the twenty-five minutes or so to where the overpass is.

I explained to the cabbie that I was writing a book and was interested to see the location from where Daniel had disappeared. That wasn't an issue to the cabbie. He was more concerned that the round trip would probably cost me in excess of $100!

'That's fine,' I told him.

It was early afternoon, and the cabbie was a friendly man in his late fifties or early sixties.

'How long have you lived here?' I asked.

'Just over ten years,' he told me. 'Moved up here from Sydney.'

'Ever regret the move?'

'Not a chance in hell! 'That's Maroochydore over there by the way,' the cabbie added referring to some high-rise buildings on the horizon in the distance.

I knew it was Maroochydore because I'd been there before, but I didn't say anything.

We turned off the main highway and onto a major arterial road.

'It's really eerie in the area around the bus stop where Daniel disappeared from,' the cabbie told me.

'Eerie in what way?' I asked.

I was more than interested to hear what the cabbie had to say, what description he might give, what words he'd use to describe the area around the bus stop where Daniel had disappeared. Obviously the area would be eerie because of what had happened! But I often discovered that regular everyday people, particularly locals to the area of a crime, would often trigger off a psychic lead for me by making a casual but instinctive comment about a case.

'I guess it's eerie because it happened in the day,' the cabbie finally said. 'I mean, how does someone nab a kid like Daniel Morcombe on a busy highway in broad daylight?'

It was a Sunday afternoon on 7 December 2003, when 13-year-old Daniel Morcombe was waiting to catch the 1.42 pm bus to the Sunshine Plaza Shopping Centre on Queensland's Sunshine Coast so he could buy Christmas presents and get a haircut. As he'd done many times before, Daniel walked the kilometre to the bus stop, and would have got there around 1.30 pm. Police say he walked towards the old Bruce Highway, or the Nambour Connection Road as it's now known. Daniel was wearing a red T-shirt with the word Billabong printed on the front, dark knee length shorts, white socks and light coloured Globe shoes. He was carrying a distinctive fob style watch. It's engraved with the word Dan.

Daniel also had a wallet containing around $150 cash, a Phone card and a school ID. Witnesses observed a blue car on the Palmwoods side of the highway with a male person leaning against the back of the car.

Composite drawings of the blue car as seen by eyewitnesses

Daniel then crossed the highway and was under the Kiel Mountain Road overpass where locals take shelter to hail buses. The overpass is located approximately 2 kilometres north of the Big Pineapple. A number of witnesses saw Daniel when he was waiting for the bus. They saw him on occasions by himself, and also standing by a blue vehicle and speaking with two male persons.

Unbeknownst to Daniel, the 1.42 pm bus had broken down. Sun Bus, who run the service have a policy of sending two replacement buses if the original has broken down. The first bus is sent to pick up the people on the broken-down bus, and won't stop for new passengers. The second bus picks up new passengers along the way. So the replacement bus passed Daniel but didn't stop to pick him up. The driver of that bus radioed to the second bus that 'a boy' was waiting at the bus stop. But by the time the second bus came along a few minutes later, Daniel was gone. He was last seen at approximately 2.10 pm under the Kiel Mountain Road overpass.

In late 2004 police released three sketches of a man seen standing behind Daniel at the bus stop before he was abducted. The man was seen leaning against the wall of the overpass as they drove past and is described as aged between twenty-five and thirty-five years, with a *lean to muscular build, He is about 175cm tall, with a gaunt face, dark brown wavy hair, goatee beard and a weathered complexion.*

The release of the artist's sketches was considered the biggest development in the investigation into Daniel's suspected murder since his disappearance a year earlier. To ensure the accuracy of the images, police had spent eleven months completing them. About 8,600 pieces of new information followed the release of the sketches, but no arrests were made. Police also had a number of witnesses who saw two men in the area at the time and believe these two people may be able to help them with their investigation.

(**) The first to sketches are very similar to Brett Cowan.

To my right, the taxi passed a new housing development where the land had been cleared. To my left were dense trees and scrub left untouched (so far) by progress, and a couple of bronzed, bare-chested teenagers entered the scrub carrying a large cage. An uncle of mine used to catch yabbies and crabs on the River Murray in a similar looking cage when I was a kid, so I figured that's what these two teenagers were doing.

A few more turns later and we were back on the main highway and passing the Big Pineapple.

'The overpass is just ahead,' the cabbie told me.

A minute or so later the Kiel Mountain Overpass loomed.

The cabbie slowed down as we passed under it, and there was a clearing on the other side where he was able to pull over.

'Just a sec,' said the cabbie. 'I'll turn around.'

When there was a break in the traffic we u-turned across the highway and drove a hundred or so metres back to the overpass. The cabbie parked underneath, right at the place where Daniel had last been seen. The first thing I noted on a psychic level was how this location looked *exactly* the same as I'd seen in the dream I'd had about Daniel when I was in New Zealand!

'Where's the sign to say this is a bus stop?' I asked the cabbie.

'There isn't one,' he told me. 'This became an unofficial bus stop after more and more locals asked to be dropped off and picked up here.'

I got out of the taxi and the traffic sped past in two double lanes of traffic either way. I stood on a large patch of hardened dirt that had been flattened by the buses and other vehicles which regularly pulled over here, and I saw a memorial to Daniel. It stands about a metre high and has a plaque which talks about Daniel, the circumstances surrounding his disappearance, and how much he is loved and missed.

Daniel's Memorial Plaque

Flowers had been left on and around the memorial, along with photos of Daniel. At the memorial's base were four small model trucks. I wondered if they were Daniel's and if he used to play with them.

I shivered.

It was a beautiful blue-sky, April day, with the temperature hovering around twenty-eight degrees. But a strong wind was blowing and it was cold standing in the shadow of the Kiel Mountain overpass. I turned from the memorial and took in the area to the other side of the highway under the overpass. The blue car had first been seen parked over there on a similar patch of hardened dirt like I was standing on. It had later been seen parked where I was standing now. In the dream I'd had about Daniel, the car that he was driven away in looked just like a friends 1989 Subaru Leone GL 1.8 Litre. Was that the car that Daniel was taken in?

(**) No. Brett Cowan was driving a white four wheel drive. The blue Leone was driven by another suspect.

Police composite of suspect car   1989 *Subaru Leone GL 1.8*

I visualised how Daniel would have crossed the highway to where I was standing. I assumed he would have had to have cut diagonally across the highway rather than in front of me where the traffic speed through, because there was a crash barrier where the lanes converged under the overpass, and there's really no space for a person to cross safely.

Satisfied with what I'd sensed at the overpass, it was time to head back to Caloundra. I'd resume my psychic detective work the following day under my own steam in the hire car.

'Thanks for showing me this,' I said as I got back into the taxi.

'No problem,' smiled the cabbie. 'Find what you're looking for?'

'Yeah,' I said as I closed the taxi door and glanced at Daniel's memorial again. 'Yeah, I think I did.' I reached for the seatbelt and buckled up. 'There'll be a sign if I'm on the right track. I'll see something, or something will happen.'

'Like what,' asked the cabbie as he looked over his shoulder to check the flow of traffic.

'Some kind of synchronicity,' I answered as the taxi made its way back onto the highway. 'A truck will drive past us with the name Daniel emblazoned on it. Something like that. Stranger things have happened.'

We were a good half hour away from the overpass when an image came to mind.

'I need to ask you something,' I told the cabbie.

'And what's that?' he asked.

'Aside from the caravan parks, and there's heaps of them up this way, is there like a … hmm, I'm not sure the best way to describe it but, is there like a shanty town or some little place close to the overpass where itinerant or poor people would live or hang out. You know, a dumpy kind of place with one shop and lots of trees.'

'By "close" to the overpass, how far are you talking?' asked the cabbie.

'Fifteen, twenty minutes.'

'Well, nothing immediately springs to mind, but I'm sure there would be a place like that around Palmwoods and the overpass. Some of the outer areas around suburbia are quite isolated, and yeah, there's lots of trees.'

'There's not a place … one word, something-o … like Rainbow or Ludo.'

'Doesn't ring a bell,' said the cabbie.

(**) *It would turn out to be the town of Eudlo.*

We were surrounded by traffic on a busy highway, and the taxi started chugging. Now I'm not mechanically minded in the least, but I deduced the taxi was suddenly besieged by engine or transmission problems!

'Doesn't sound good,' I commented.

'No it doesn't,' frowned the cabbie. 'I don't know what it could be. It's just been serviced.

The chugging grew worse, so the cabbie moved the taxi into the left lane as someone tooted their horn and sped past us, annoyed that the taxi was slowing traffic.

'This is a first time for me,' the cabbie told me as he moved the transmission from first to second to see if it made any difference.

It did, but the problem became worse!

'I've never had anything like this happen before,' the cabbie told me.

I didn't tell him that I felt this was a sign that I was on the right track, because I didn't want to freak him out. Daniel's bus had broken down, and now the taxi was breaking down and right at the moment I was trying to figure out the name of a town. Was that because Daniel had been taken to that town?

(**) *Yes, he and Cowan drove through Eudlo.*

The cabbie steered the taxi into a side lane and it came to one last shuddering, final stop. Over and over the cabbie tried to get the engine started, but it resisted every attempt. Without the engine running and no air conditioning, it quickly became very hot inside the taxi, so I got out as the cabbie made a call on his two-way. A couple of guys in their early twenties gave a hand pushing the taxi to the side of the highway so that it wasn't obstructing traffic.

'Thanks fella's!' the cabbie said after steering the vehicle to safety.

'No problem mate!' one of them replied. Then he and his mate wandered off towards some local shops where a teenage girl was leaning against a car waiting for them.

'Daniel! Shift your arse!' she called out. 'We'll be late!'

And just to top off the eventful synchronicities and spiritual signs, they drove away in a blue car!

The next day in my hire car I cruised around Maroochydore to see if anything caught my attention visually or spiritually, and to check out a couple of specific addresses including the Sunshine Shopping Centre. Satisfied with what I sensed at those locations, I moved on to other areas in and around Coolum, seeing what I felt, looking for synchronicities. I was also very keen to sort out the caravan connection to Daniel's case. Since my time in New Zealand I'd been drawn to the image of the caravan in the photo of the Crawford house rather than the house itself. So I knew it was the caravan that I was meant to take most notice of.

(**) *Caravans would feature strongly throughout Brett Cowan's criminal and personal history, which is why I had so many images and questions about caravans.*

Had Daniel been taken to a small town where the perpetrator lived in a caravan?

Had Daniel been taken to a house with a caravan parked out the front, or in the driveway?

Had Daniel been taken to a location at or near a caravan park?

Did someone living in a caravan innocently see something the day Daniel disappeared?

These were the questions I asked myself as I drove in around Maroochydore, keeping my eyes peeled for any caravan that stood out to me.

I later discovered that Police had conducted DNA tests on residents from caravan parks throughout southeast Queensland in the hunt for clues to the disappearance of Daniel. Detectives took swabs from people living in 63 caravan parks, stretching from

Redcliffe across the Sunshine Coast to Gympie. Police hoped the tests would help them determine who was in the vicinity of the bus stop that Daniel disappeared from. Many people from the Woombye Gardens Caravan Park use the bus stop.

I checked the Woombye Gardens Caravan Park out but didn't sense much feeling from that location. But the Coolum Caravan Park *did* have a huge spiritual energy around it!

While I don't believe that Daniel was taken to the Coolum Caravan Park there, I do believe a tourist who was staying there saw something at, or near the overpass concerning Daniel. I believe they headed back interstate a day or so later, and not being familiar with the Kiel Mountain Overpass area, nor hearing a lot of the media news about Daniel (because there wasn't nearly as much about him interstate as there was in Queensland), and they haven't made the connection that they are a valuable witness. I have the name Terry or Terrence, can be first or last name.

I was also looking for the house that I'd seen in the dream that the little girl had taken me to…

(**) *It was the secluded house that Cowan had taken Daniel to as described in Chapter 10.*

"Across the countryside I flew, and as I crested a tree-lined hill, the lights of a country town appeared ahead to my left, and the lights of a city were further on in the distance to my right. I veered towards an area in between the lights of the country town and the city, and I slowly descended, gently landing on a dirt road that passed in front of an older style house. No lights were on in the house. It looked ominous and foreboding!

Why am I here again? I wondered.

What is it they want me to see?"

The little girl and Daniel wanted me to see the tree-lined location and house where Daniel was taken and murdered. The "lights of a country town" turned out to be those of nearby Beerwah, and the "lights of a city" in the other direction, while not geographically close, were symbolically those of Brisbane.

I was going to check out a secluded and supposedly haunted house in the area that a journalist friend had told me about, I'd been sent interior and exterior footage of the house taken during the day, and while it didn't look like the house that the little girl had taken me to, my journo friend was certain that, 'a lot of weird shit had gone down there. Check out if you feel Daniel was taken to this house,' the journo told me. 'Other psychics believe he could have been.'

As I leant against the hire car outside the property where the house was, I didn't sense any of Daniel's energy there whatsoever, although I did agree that the energy coming from the house was quite dark, and that someone had probably come to grief there at some stage. But I couldn't think about that now. I had to stay focussed on Daniel.

And why did I always *see* Bribie Island when I thought about Daniel? Bribie Island was maybe a forty-five minutes drive south (back towards Brisbane) from where I was now. I'd been to Bribie Island only once for a barbecue with friends some years before, and didn't have time to drive down there again on this trip. But I vividly remembered a bridge I drove across when leaving Bribie Island and a view of the Glass House Mountains in the distance.

Whenever I thought of Daniel, I saw that image. Somewhere, somehow, it was connected.

The Glass House Mountains viewed from Bribie Island

(**) *Brett Cowan took Daniel to the Glass House Mountains and murdered him at an isolated house there.*

On the flight home I thought about how Lochie and Daniel had appeared in a dream together. Had the same person or people taken them, even though they'd disappeared thirteen years apart? Were they together in spirit because of their common love of motocross and trail bikes? I mulled over a number of possible scenarios on the flight home, and wanted to clear up one line of thinking regarding Daniel's disappearance.

The person who would help me do that was Tom, a senior student at my karate club. Now in his late twenties, Tom had often told me how as a youngster he was passionate about go-kart racing. Once a week, Tom and I go for a brisk five to eight kilometre walk to discuss everything that's going on at the karate club, and what we plan to do in the following week as far as training goes. It was on one of these walks after my return from Queensland that I casually ran a few questions past Tom without telling him why I was asking them.

'Tom, you've told me about your passion for go-karting when you were a kid. What did being involved with go-karting mean to you?'

'Well,' Tom replied. 'It was an intense focus of my energies and I can't explain exactly where it came from. It's just something I really wanted to do almost to the point of it being an obsession!'

'What steps did you take to be involved with it?'

'Well,' Tom began, 'it was a gradual process. I decided when I was ten that it was something that I wanted to do, so I began saving. And even though it took me five years, by the time I was fifteen I bought my first crappy, second-hand go-cart. And I loved it!'

'Did you ever have friendships with people that your parents didn't know about?'

'Sure. I had friends at the go-kart track that I'd see week to week who my parents didn't meet, friends who I'd go up to and say hello.'

'So you spoke to these people on a regular basis?

'Yes.'

'And you were how old?'

'Fifteen.'

'Tom, now that you're a few years older and can look at your situation back then with a more mature perspective, did you ever see these friends on your own, or place yourself in what you might now view as a precarious situation?'

Tom took a drink from his water bottle as he pondered that question. 'You know,' he began, 'some of the friendships I had you might have called unorthodox. And looking back on it now I can see how my parents might have seen it as strange that I had friendships with people up to three times my age, and that I felt like I had a common bond with them. It was just I was so passionate about go-karting that I cultivated friendships with a lot of different people. I had a mate called Bill who was at least in his sixties. I met him at the go-cart track and spoke regularly to him on the phone. I also ended up playing golf with him, and Mum only met him for the first time one day when he came to pick me up to go and play golf together. I considered Bill to be a good mate.

'How old were you then?' I asked.

'I was still at school, so I would have probably been fifteen or sixteen.'

Tom is now a psychologist, so he certainly has the mental goods to be level headed. From what I'd read in newspaper articles, been told by journo's, and learnt from Daniel's spiritual profile, he too was very level-headed. But when we're young and passionate about something, when we're still naively trusting no matter what our upbringing, do we still take chances or enter situations we shouldn't?

Tom did, I certainly did, and maybe Daniel did too!

(**) *Yes, Daniel did.*

'Tom, if you missed your bus and bumped into some of the older guy's from go-karting, and they offered you a lift, would you have gone with them?'

'Well, there were a couple of guys who were as bit dodgy, you know, rough and drank too much, but most of them, yes. I would have accepted a lift from them.'

'Did you ever accept a lift with any of them?'

'Well, yes.'

When I checked out Daniel's spiritual profile, there was nothing that showed me he would have gone with a stranger.

(**) Cowan told police that Daniel willingly got into his four-wheel drive because he believed he'd missed his bus.

I also don't believe that Daniel would have allowed himself to get physically close enough to a stranger so that they could bundle him into their car. And considering the busy stretch of highway where Daniel was taken, if that was attempted, the traffic is so busy through there that someone driving past would have seen a scuffle going on.

(**) Cowan and Daniel casually walked a few metres away out of sight from the highway to where Cowan had parked his four-wheel drive.

The strongest feeling I have is that no matter how Daniel got into the car, the person or persons connected to the blue car were familiar to him in some way, more than likely through his love of motocross, and so his guard was down. Daniel may not have known these people very well, perhaps only in passing, but enough to take a lift with them when the scheduled bus didn't pick him up.

Was Daniel given a lift under the pretence of going to the Sunshine Shopping Centre, but lured to check out some bikes at a private dwelling, perhaps a caravan, along the way?

(**) The trail bike scenario actually turned out to be something from Brett Cowan's past. Cowan was nine-years-old when he sexually assaulted his first child. He'd let children ride with him on his pushbike and then assault them. He'd later do the same as a teenager using a ride on his trail bike as a ploy.

Two significant places of interest on a spiritual level are the Coolum Caravan Park and the small, secluded town of Eudlo about ten kilometres south of the Kiel Mountain Overpass.

(**) *Cowan once stayed at the Coolum Caravan Park. As for Eudlo, Cowan drove Daniel south through Eudlo and on to the Glass House Mountains, a distance of thirty-two kilometres.*

There's also a sister or ex-girlfriend of one of the perpetrators who is wracked with guilt over her knowledge of what happened. There are two names associated with this lady: Ellen or Ellie. There are also the male names of Arnie or Arnold.

(**) *Cowan carried out violent, sexual fantasies on the women he dated. One of his ex-girlfriends was the first to figure out that Cowan had killed Daniel. She said that she carried the guilt and the secret for years. One of the partners name's was Tracy. Another girlfriend was Elly.*

This woman and man have not come forward with information, and have solid knowledge that could help prosecute a suspect I sense the Queensland police are keeping tabs on because they believe he took Daniel.

(**) *After Cowan's arrest it was revealed that undercover police had lived alongside him at a Perth caravan park. Cowan was arrested following a sophisticated undercover sting that ended with him leading police to Daniel's remains. In August 2011, two shoes and three human bones confirmed to be Daniel's were found at a search site at the Glass House Mountains.*

Daniel Morcombe.

Brett Cowan

Cowan confessed to offering Daniel a lift to the Sunshine Plaza Shopping Centre in December 2003.

'He got willingly into the car because he missed the bus. He jumped in, front passenger seat. Didn't talk much at all. I said, "I've just gotta duck home quickly and let me missus know what was goin' on". That's why we were goin' down the hill and not straight ahead. I had no intention of going anywhere near my wife. "Yeah",

he said. 'I took him to a secluded spot that I knew of,' Cowan confessed to police. 'The end of Roys Road comes in here to a macadamia or an avocado farm. I actually went into the house there while he sat in the car. You know, to make it look good I went in and then came back out. And then I said, "oh me missus said come in and get a drink". He came inside and I went to pull his pants down, he panicked and I grabbed him. I never got to molest him or anything like that, he panicked and I panicked and grabbed him around the throat and before I knew it he was dead. There was no screaming or nothing. Choked him. I didn't (molest) him. I didn't get a chance to.

Where I put his body and everything is an old sand mine. You know twelve-year-old, ya can pick up a twelve-year-old an' throw him. There's an embankment. It's all been grown over with trees and bush. Took him out of the car. Threw him down there. Then got down there myself and I dragged him over. I don't know how far it was. He had all his clothes on then. I've stripped him off. I didn't bury him, I just put him under branches and shit. His clothes I took back with me.

There's a creek there that was fast flowing and I threw his clothes in there. Just threw 'em all in. They sank and floated away. It was ten to fifteen minutes and I was back in the car and driving back home. Within that week, I went back. Just in case, I went and took a shovel back. Went down to where I put him and I only found a fragment of bone. The rest of it was gone. There's a lot of yabbies and animals and that sort of thing. I think that was part of the skull. I just buried it in there. Like, broke it up with a shovel. That's all that was left.'

In 1987 at the age of eighteen, Cowan snatched a young boy from a playgroup, took him into a toilet block and repeatedly raped him. He was sentenced to two years jail and served just fourteen months.

In 1993 while living in a caravan park on the outskirts of Darwin, Cowan raped, suffocated and left a six-year-old boy for dead. The boy stumbled into a petrol station some time later, naked, filthy, covered in blood and barely able to breathe. He had blood blisters on his face, broken blood vessels in his eyes, a punctured lung, severe lacerations and injuries consistent with violent sexual abuse. The boy's injuries were so severe police expected him to die. Cowan was arrested and charged, and despite having been previously jailed for raping another child, he was only given a seven-year jail term and then released after serving four years.

Cowan had also been the target of a revenge attack by the brothers of a fourteen-year-old girl he was accused of raping. In 2008 the brothers tried to ambush Cowan by calling for a tow truck, but the wrong driver showed up. The driver was beaten with a wrench until the men realized they had the wrong person. They told the young driver they had planned to kill Cowan.

Cowan told police and his mother he was never abused and offered no explanation for his actions.

Because of his criminal history, police spoke to Cowan shortly after Daniel's abduction. At the time Cowan admitted to driving past the Kiel Mountain Road overpass when Daniel would have been waiting for a bus. He denied seeing Daniel and forensic examinations conducted on his car found nothing. Police were also contacted by numerous people who said sketches and computer generated images of a suspect seen standing behind Daniel at the bus stop looked just like Cowan.

On March 13, 2014, Cowan was found guilty of the murder of Daniel Morcombe. He was sentenced to life in prison.

Daniel's father Bruce Morcombe said, "I felt he was a remarkably simple person to identify and this was a simple puzzle to solve."

On December 7, 2012, thousands turned out for Daniel Morcombe's funeral As the Morcombe family walked behind Daniel's white casket adorned with red flowers, hundreds joined an honor guard formed by students at his former school.

The Honor Guard at Daniel's funeral.

When the coffin neared the end of the honor line, State Emergency Service volunteers stood to attention beside the hearse. The impromptu display of solidarity with the Morcombe's brought tears to those watching on, and as the hearse pulled out of the school grounds the crowd broke into quiet applause. 'A moment in time that will live with all of us forever occurred nine years ago today,' Bruce Morcombe said at the funeral. 'Appreciate that the evil act which took Daniel happened a long time ago. Today is about embracing his return to family and being reflective of what might have been.

I'm sure we have all discovered strengths we did not know we had.'

The Morcombe family at Daniel's funeral.

'Australia is a better place because of this. Our children and grandchildren are safer because of Daniel's legacy. What is truly ironic about all the recognition, support, help and publicity his search has attracted is that he was such a quiet kid. He was not an attention seeker yet because of his sparkling eyes and beaming smile captured in photo after photo he is someone everyone took into their hearts. That is what made him special!'

For nine years, the Christmas presents Denise and Bruce Morcombe bought their son Daniel remained unopened, a permanent reminder of their little boy who went out and never returned. As they laid him to rest the Morcombe's were at last be able to give Daniel his gifts, placing them on his coffin before saying their goodbyes.

Chapter 20

DETECTIVE SWAN

There wasn't a breath of wind.

There wasn't a noise.

There wasn't a colour.

There was just darkness and the isolation of the desert.

The little girl in the pink dress was playing hopscotch on the bitumen road beside me. This dream was familiar. I'd had it before.

'You shouldn't be playing on the road,' I told her. 'What if a car comes?'

'Uncle Peter will look after me,' she giggled as she jumped from square to square.

'Yes I will,' I heard a voice say, 'I will always look after her.' I peered into the darkness, and couldn't see anyone at first, but then Peter Falconio stepped forward and stood next to where the little girl was playing.'

'I'm almost ready Uncle Peter,' the little girl said.

'That's okay,' said Peter, 'but as soon as you're finished we need to get going.'

With that the little girl finished one more turn of going up and down the hopscotch squares. She jumped out of the final square, landed at Peter's feet, and looked up at him smiling.

'I'm ready,' she said. 'Where are we going Uncle Peter?'

'A beautiful place,' Peter replied. 'The desert is your home little one.'

"The desert is your home little one". I'd heard those words before. That's right, the elder at the campfire. He'd said those words to the little girl when she was hiding behind the rocks.

"The desert is your home little one" - around and around in my mind those words spun, and suddenly a possible name of who the little girl might be came to me. I tossed it around for a moment and felt ludicrous to even consider it. But I also knew from experience that if I tried to reason things through too much, that I'd go off the trail.

I took a chance.

Peter and the little girl had turned and were walking into the desert away from me.

'Azaria?' I said.

They stopped walking, and the little girl in the pink dress turned around and beamed a huge confirming smile.

'Azaria,' she said. The little girl placed her hand on her chest above her heart. 'I am here, and I give my mummy and my daddy big hugs and kisses everyday!'

The little girl walked over to me and put her arms up so that I'd pick her up. I did, and hugged her tightly. I closed my eyes and felt a surge of spiritual energy, tingling, warm, and peaceful. I opened my eyes to discover that I was now holding a sleeping baby surrounded by shimmering blue light. This little baby was how Azaria had looked the few short weeks that she'd been alive. How she showed herself from spirit is how she would have looked if she'd lived - and "the little girl" was how she wanted to be seen, and remembered, a joyous giggler who liked to run and have fun just like every other kid.

'Can I hold her?' I heard someone say from behind me.

I turned to see Lochie, standing there with his arms reaching out to me.

'Of course,' I said, and I gently handed him Azaria.

Lochie looked to her adoringly, and then looked up to me.

'I look after her too,' he said. 'We all look after each other here in spirit.'

'We all look after each other here in spirit,' I heard another voice repeat.

Just behind Lochie, a female spirit stepped into view.

It was Jane Beaumont.

'Tell him,' she told me.

'Tell who?' I asked.

I was woken by someone knocking at the door. It was early afternoon and I'd fallen asleep on the lounge. I groggily walked from the lounge to the door and when I answered, a man dressed very formally with a tie, and holding a folder, greeted me.

'Scott Russell Hill?'

'That's right.'

'Detective Sergeant Brian Swan, S.A. Police,' he announced as he held up his identification.

Detective Sergeant Swan's visit was completely out of the blue. There hadn't been any phone call or pre-warning that he was coming. And I can hear the jokesters saying, 'Ah, but you're psychic, you should have known!' But as I always say, just because I'm psychic doesn't mean I know everything. And because of the overall negativity that police have towards psychics, a visit from Detective Sergeant Swan or any policeman was the furthest thing from my mind.

'Well Brian,' I said with surprise as I held the door open. 'I didn't think that you and I would ever cross paths.'

'Why would you think that?' he asked as he walked inside.

'Because I heard that you don't think much of psychics, that we make you angry.'

'Well that's not true,' Brian said. 'I've encountered many situations, and I certainly believe that some people are very intuitive, so I wouldn't say that I'm a sceptic.'

After initial pleasantries, Brian told me about his involvement with the Beaumont Case after he took it over from another policeman years earlier. He told me how he has built a friendship with Jim and Nancy Beaumont, that they catch up for coffee every now and then, and that he's very protective of them, especially in shielding them from the media.

Brian then moved into giving examples of where psychics had contacted the police.

'What would you say to this?' he asked me, before revealing what a couple of different psychics had told police. What Brian was really referring to in asking me what I thought, was not so much about what the psychics had said (because it was non-specific and generally unhelpful information), but to see how I'd feel if I was on the receiving end of such information. It was his way of getting me to see the difficulties that the police come up against in dealing with visions instead of facts. I did, of course, already understand that difficulty, but I appreciated his position in needing to reinforce that to me.

Then Brian veered off the psychic issue and gave me some examples where, especially on January 26th each year (the anniversary of the Beaumont children's disappearance) people's memories are jolted and they come forward with information they've just remembered.

Overall though, he was hitting home to me what I was well aware of; that the police need to deal in facts, and I agreed with him on that. But I also talked about the other side of the coin, that when all the facts aren't there that surely the police must act on intuition or hunches, that they would put together scenarios to try and find the missing pieces to a case. I actually believe that many police are quite psychic.

We then moved on to an article from a January 2006 *Woman's Day* magazine which featured a story about me and a headline reading: "I know where the Beaumont Children are". Brian had the article attached to a clipboard, and told me how members of the public had brought the article to the attention of police.

'So how do you think we should react to this?' Brian asked.

'Well, you're here!' was all I could think of to say.

And then it was over to me. Brian took notes, listened intently, and didn't react to anything that I told him. I began by talking about my childhood in Glenelg and my personal memories of the Beaumont family, and Brian asked an occasional question to verify a point I was making. I then told him how the children's disappearance had affected me, and how passionate I was about uncovering some new leads that might help solve the case. I also passed on all the information about the Beaumont Children featured in this book, plus specific names and addresses of people living in and around Glenelg at the time which are not included (for privacy reasons).

Brian told me he knew the Glenelg area well, especially its history and what it was like in 1966 when he was a young constable. He knew many of the stables that were there then; including one the police had searched for drugs.

But here's the thing, Brian said. 'Say you live at for example, 21 Smith Street, and I knock on your day and say, hello, I'm Brian Swan from the South Australian Police, and we have information that the Beaumont Children are buried in your backyard. How would you react to that?'

'I don't think it's about digging up backyards anymore Brain,' I answered. 'I think it's about getting people to talk. People who know what happened to the Beaumont Children are still alive, and it's about finding them and putting the pressure on so that someone will speak up and reveal exactly what happened. Maybe someone on the list I've given you *is* that person!'

'The Beaumont Case is no longer a full time investigation, Brian told me as he stood up to leave after a two hour visit. 'But in amongst everything else I do, I'll check what you've given me, and I'll get back to you.'

'Thank you Brian,' I said as we shook hands. 'I'm relieved that I've been able to speak to you. And I appreciate it.'

I closed the front door after Brian left and let out a grateful sigh. From the time I was a little kid when the Beaumont children disappeared through to now as an adult, I'd gone full circle in my quest to shine new light on the Beaumont mystery. That my information was now in the hands of the police was a satisfying conclusion to many years of effort, and I felt more than ready to let the Case go so I could move away from psychic detective work and on to new challenges.

Both on *Sensing Murder* and privately I worked on the Cases to try and bring closure to the families, to bring a possible breakthrough to each Case, and to set a new standard of what psychic work could achieve. Along the way I was constantly reminded of something I already knew; that those on the other side never leave us.

Speak *out loud* and they will hear you.

Speak *within* and hear yourself.

Chapter 21

Beaumont Children - 2015 Update

In May 2013, seven years after the original release of *Psychic Detective*, I received an email from a man called Stuart Mullins. Stuart was a former Adelaide resident now living in Queensland, and his email explained that he'd been privately financing an investigation into the missing Beaumont children.

'I have a former Major Crime detective working with me on the case,' Stuart's email said. 'His name's Bill Hayes and he'd love to talk to you. Would it be possible to set up a meeting?'

This could be interesting was my initial thought because this wasn't the usual deluded email I receive about the Beaumont children. Only recently I'd received an email from a man in Sydney who claimed he was Grant Beaumont. The fact this man was ten years too young to be Grant Beaumont was beside the point. He was determined he was Grant and was quite offended when I didn't buy into his story!

What did put me off thought was that Stuart Mullins mentioned in his email that he was helping research a book by an author named Alan Whitiker. Whitiker had contacted me a few years earlier for my possible input into his book titled *Finding the Beaumont Children*. I sent back a very nice email explaining that I was under contractual obligation with *Woman's Day* magazine at the time and couldn't speak to anyone but the magazine about my findings on the Beaumont case. Well Whitiker obviously didn't like my response because he went on to write in his book that I'd turned down his request and must obviously be a charlatan.

'Forget about all that!' My PA Kerstin told me. 'What Stuart's proposing sounds very interesting. Why don't you give him a call.'

So the next day as I drove to karate training I made the call and found Stuart to be a very nice man. Being originally from Adelaide, the Beaumont case had always haunted him, and like so many people he wanted it resolved.

'Anything I can do to help make that happen, I'll do,' Stuart told me. 'And Bill Hayes is really keen to speak to you Scott. We think you can help.'

'In what way?' I asked.

'We have a specific location of where we think the children might be,' Stuart told me. 'We're wondering if you might be able to give us more information on that. We also feel we know who took the children and we're looking for your thoughts on that about that too.'

'And what will you do with that information?' I asked.

'Well we have contacts at *A Current Affair* and *Today Tonight*, so they're tracking the story with is and will feature it soon. We also have a book coming out soon about our findings.'

'By Alan Whitiker your email said.'

'That's right.'

'I'm not a fan of his,' I said bluntly. 'He slagged me in his last book.'

Stuart didn't reply right away.

Then…

'Yes, I'm aware of that,' Stuart told me, 'but is it possible for us to move away from that now and try and bring the Beaumont case to some kind of resolution…together?'

It was my turn not to reply right away.

Then…

Well I'll tell you something Stuart,' I said. 'A friend of mine works at a pub at Glenelg. And she told me how the other week there was recently an elderly lady sitting at the bar. The lady was crying. When my friend asked what was wrong the elderly lady told her she was crying because she missed her children. Stuart, the lady at the bar was Nancy Beaumont. And it was Nancy who told me many years ago that I was here to do some very special things. I intend to do that.'

'So you're in?' Stuart asked.

'I'm in,' I confirmed.

Bill Hayes knocked on my front door at 4pm two days later. The former Major Crime detective was a tall man in his late 50's or early 60's, and had a shiny bald head. He was genuinely friendly, and most appreciative to speak to me.

'Stuart says you do karate,' Bill said as we sat down in my living room.

'That's right.'

'Me too,' Bill smiled. 'I still love to train.'

'And how long have you been working on the Beaumont case?' I asked.

'Oh privately about four years,' Bill told me, 'but there were areas of the case I looked into when I was on the force.'

'Why such an interest now?' I asked.

'Well,' Bill began, 'there's the obvious reason of course. It happened here and is probably our countries most famous unsolved case. And also because there's those of us who know there's been some gaps in the investigation over the years, some errors, some areas that could have been handled better. It's time to try and fix that. There needs to be a Royal Commission into the Beaumont case, a proper investigation into everything that's happened over the years. That's what we're hoping for.'

'And what do your mates who are still on the force think of what you're doing?' I asked.

Bill smiled again. 'Well, there's some who say "good on you," because they understand why I'm doing it. But there's some who are against it, and others whose toes will be trodden on. Those guys in particular, they'll get angry, especially when I go public with our findings.'

'When are you going to do that?'

'Probably next month.'

'And what are those findings?' I asked.

Bill sighed and sat forward in his chair as he clasped his hands together.

'We believe we know who took the children and where he took them. Our case against this man is so strong you'd have to convince me it's *not* him!'

Bill went on to tell me about Harry Phipps, a rich factory owner who lived very close to where the children disappeared. Phipps liked to dress in satin women's clothing, and had been accused of sexually abusing one of his sons. The son had also claimed that he saw three children in their backyard on the day the Beaumont children disappeared.

Wealthy Harry Phipps was also well known for handing out one pound notes, and it was a one pound note that Jane Beaumont paid for the children's lunch that day when they'd gone to the beach with only six shillings and sixpence.'

The Phipps house was just a couple of streets away from Glenelg beach and within easy walking distance. Bill described Phipps as a very fit, athletic man, who spent a lot of time swimming at Glenelg beach, and who fitted one of the old identikit pictures that had been circulating since 1966.

'It's very hard to find a photo of Phipps,' Bill told me. 'It seems he avoided having his photo taken. But I do have this one taken at a work function.'

Original Identikit   Younger Harry Phipps   Older
Harry Phipps

'Scott I understand that you work with dates of birth.'
'That's right.'
Phipps has been dead for about ten years now, but if I give you his date of birth, would you be able to tell me anything about him?

'Sure. I can also tell you what he would have been working through emotionally and personally back in 1966.'

'Based on his date?'

'Based on his date,' I confirmed.

Bill handed me the date – July 1, 1917, and I studied it for a moment.

'Well,' I said, 'if you're looking for his date to be that of someone who's a straight out criminal or predator, then you're going to be disappointed because this date is actually very generous. If I step aside from what you've told me and look at this without all the negatives, Phipps was actually very well liked and genuinely loved to share his money around and help people, buy gifts, pay extra, that kind of thing.'

'That's certainly true,' Bill confirmed.

But he also loved his own space and doing his own thing. He had friends around when he wanted them, but was more than happy being on his own. If anything, he craved his own space. On the negative side of his profile, there are aspects where he could detach emotionally, especially from his wife or children, and become quite nasty, angry or violent. So to me, Phipps is a bit of a Jekyl and Hyde. There was a side of him that could be generous, caring and happy. But there was another side of Phipps that could be calculating, cold, narcissistic and hurtful.'

'That's also true,' Bill told me.

'And in 1966, his spiritual cycles show that he was working through a major cycle of uncertainty. He wanted the next step of his life and business, something new to happen. Despite his success he would have been really focussed on what areas of his life weren't working the way he wanted, and that would have made him even more edgy and detached from those around him. People can lose the plot during spiritual cycles like he was in then.'

'Lose the plot enough to take the children?' Bill asked.

'Enough to do something very daring, yes.' I confirmed.

Bill cut to the chase. 'Scott can you confirm that Phipps is our man?'

I thought about that for a moment.

'To be really honest with you Bill, no, I can't. But I tell you why. I believe that I'm just so personally close to the Beaumont case that my thinking gets cluttered with a whole lot of stuff. So while everything you've told me is very compelling and certainly sounds like you've found your guy, me being able to tell you that it's definitely him, it's just not there. Whereas it probably would be there if we were talking about another case that I wasn't personally involved with. Does that make sense?'

'I think so,' said Bill.

'It's kind of like trying to a reading for yourself,' I explained. 'You just shouldn't do it because for some reason it comes out all jumbled. But when you do a reading for someone else, it's clear.'

'So what you're basically saying is that having your personal involvement with the Beaumont case can cloud your judgement,' Bill said.

'Not so much cloud my judgement, but more it clouds what I feel to a question like, "is he our man?" I mean, I want resolution to this case so bad I'm always careful not to jump and point the finger just for the hell of it! But all the information I told you from his date of birth is separate to that. That was me tuning into his date and telling you what I feel. There's no emotional connection or cloudiness in me doing that.'

Bill nodded. 'I think I understand.'

'Maybe I can help you in a different way though,' I said.

'How so?' Bill asked.

'Well, Grant Beaumont channels a lot of information through me,' I said. 'He's often described where he and his sisters went after they were at Wenzel's cake shop, and if I described the route they took and the house they went to, you can see whether it matches what you know.'

'Sounds good,' said Bill.

And so I told Bill what Grant had shown me. I won't go into detail because other people live at the former Phipps house now. But Bill confirmed that Grant led me to Harry Phipps's house.

'You've described it all,' Bill told me. 'Right down to the garage at the back.'

'Well you can thank Grant for that,' I said. 'Does that help you with your question of whether Phipps is your guy or not?'

'Yes it does,' said Bill. 'But I do have one other question.'

'Sure.'

We believe that Phipps took the children to a factory he owned, and buried them there. Could you confirm that, or is that also too emotionally close to things for you?'

'No I think that'll be okay,' I said. 'But I'll tell you how we'll do it. Come over to my desk.'

Bill and I walked over to my desk where I do my readings and sat down.

'I'm going to use the Tarot cards as well,' I told Bill. 'Now I know that's going to seem a little out there, but just go with the flow. That's why you're here.'

'Whatever you need to do Scott,' Bill told me.

'And here's what I need you to do,' I said as I pushed a sheet of paper and pen towards Bill. 'Don't tell me anything about the factory or where it's located. Just draw a simple diagram and divide it up into sections, numbering each section from one to six. If I feel the children are there, I'll tell you the number that relates to that feeling. And I'll look away while you're drawing it so I can't see it.'

I turned away as Bill drew the map, and I shuffled the Tarot cards that my friend Veronica had given me many years earlier.

'All done,' Bill told me a few moments later.

'Turn the paper over so I can't see it,' I said.

'Okay.'

And I turned back.

'Now there's something I want to show you before I read on this,' I said. And I flipped through the cards until I found the one that represented Harry Phipps. Based on his Cancerian starsign, the card is called the *King of Cups*.

'This is Phipps's card,' I said. And I left it on the table for Bill to look at while I went through the cards and found the *Wheel of Fortune*. ' And this is the *Wheel of Fortune*, the best card in the pack and what I call the ultimate "yes" card. No other card beats it. Now, how many sections have you drawn on your map?'

'Six.'

'So I'm going to lay out six rows of five cards, and basically see whether the cards are a "yes" or a "no" to the children being in that particular section of your map. The more "yes" cards you get on any particular row, the better it is. And if Phipps's card or the *Wheel of Fortune* come up, even better. But we also might find that the cards say the children aren't at the factory.'

'Phipps's son told me the children are in a pit.'

'Well let's see what we get,' I said.

I put the *King of Cups* and the *Wheel of Fortune* back in the deck separately so they wouldn't be together.

'Now you shuffle,' I told Bill as I handed the cards to him.

Bill quietly shuffled.

When he was done…

'What now?' he asked.

'Split them into six piles.'

Which he did.

'Now which pile relates to section one of your diagram?'

Bill pondered the six piles of cards and made a selection.

'That one.'

And we worked our way through the other piles of cards allocating a number to them.

'Right,' I said once that was done. 'Let's see what we have.'

I picked up the cards that Bill had selected for section one, and laid five of the cards out in a row.

'They're not in section one,' I said.

I laid out the cards that Bill had selected for section two.

'They're not in section two.'

I laid out the cards Bill had selected for section three.

They're not in section three.'

I picked up the cards that Bill had selected for section four and laid down the first card.

It was the *King of Cups!*

Bill reacted.

'That's Phipps's card isn't it?'

'Yes it is,' I confirmed. 'Wouldn't it be amazing if the *Wheel of Fortune* came up now too.'

And with that I turned over the next card and it was the *Wheel of Fortune!*

Bill stared at what was before him. I could see he was quite taken back by it.

'You separated those two cards before you put them back in the pack,' Bill said. 'I watched you do it.'

'Welcome to my world,' I said. 'Bill, they're in section four. We don't have to do the other cards. With Phipps's card there and the *Wheel of Fortune* as the ultimate "yes", that's it!'

Bill looked to me. 'Section 4 is where the pit is. That's where we think the children are.'

I looked to Bill. 'Grant's telling me that he and his sisters were separated and moved around a couple of times after they'd passed. They may not be together.'

'Well it's time to find out,' Bill told me, 'because something's in that pit that's for sure!'

A month later Bill did an interview on TV's *A Current Affair*. It stirred up a hornet's nest in the media. The following night *Today Tonight* did the first of three or four stories on the Beaumont case and Bill's investigations, and the story turned from a hornet's nest into a wildfire! The continuing public comment was, "why didn't the police know this already?" And the police response was highly critical, saying that Bill was digging up information that had been looked at in years past and had come to nothing.

'A lot of bullets are being fired your way,' I said to Bill on the phone one morning.

'He chuckled. 'Well Scott, I've been shot at for real,' Bill told me, 'so I can handle a volley of personal attacks!'

The TV stories brought two brothers forward. Both now professional men in the 60's, their father had once worked at the factory Phipps owned. The brothers told *Today Tonight* that while they were on school holidays in January 1966 (when the Beaumont children disappeared), Phipps had asked them to dig a large hole at the rear of his factory. The boys were only teenagers at the time, and even though the work was hard they said that Phipps paid them well and once they were finished they heard no more about it. Over the years they would occasionally recount the story of the "strange man (Phipps) who watched us dig that hole."

In November 2013, and with public pressure mounting, police checked the factory grounds with ground-penetrating radar and then excavated a "small piece of land", but no remains of the Beaumont children were found. The three square metre site they excavated was where the brothers said they'd dug the hole for Harry Phipps.

The excavated area *wasn't* Section 4 of Bill's map!

Police Commissioner Paul Dickson told a press conference:

'As we all know, our Major Crime Investigation Branch is a very professional group of police officers. This year they've had a number of successes, and in particular they've had two successes relating to long-standing investigations. Those investigations have come to a resolution stage only because of their professionalism and commitment, and the real belief which all police officers have that no case is ever closed until it comes to the resolution stage. And that's where we're with the Beaumont investigation. Until we actually resolve the matter successfully, it won't be closed. This part of the investigation is completed today, but we will always look at further information that comes to us.

Commissioner Paul Dickson at the press conference

I think it's really important that I strongly refute the unwarranted and unsubstantiated statements calling to question the professionalism of our Major Crime Investigation Branch. They are clearly unfounded. And to be quite frank, without the media interest in this, we probably would have never searched that premises, but because the media interest created concern into the community, we always evaluate what we should do. In this case it was appropriate and that's what we did, but in other circumstances we may not have done that.'

'Are you confident you can rule that area out completely?' asks a reporter.

'We are, yes.'

'Did you use ground penetrating radar within other areas of the factory?'

'We did.'

'And what's been the response today from the Beaumont family?'

We've been with the Beaumont family all day. Our victim contact officer was with her (Nancy) through the whole exercise to support her, to provide her with continual briefing of what's happening. And that contact will continue into the future. There's no doubt that this whole event has raised concerns with the family. They are very supportive of the actions of the police and we will continue with that. Unfortunately this is a very long and evolved investigation, and it does take a lot of hurt and pain for the family.

Epilogue

A month later Christmas arrived, a New Year began, and the resurgence of hype around the Beaumont case was suddenly over. A Royal Commission never eventuated, yet.

In 2014, I met some friends of Harry Phipps who were outraged by the accusations levelled at him.

'He was such a lovely man,' I was told. 'He would never have taken the children!'

All of Bill Hayes findings are in Alan Whitiker and Stuart Mullins book, *The Satin Man.* Those who have read it say it's an incredibly thought provoking and compelling read.

As I write this, the 50th anniversary of the Beaumont children is approaching. It will come around on January 26, 2016. Whether you read this before or after that date, please take a moment to remember my friends Jane, Arnna and Grant. They were three regular kids who went to the beach one day and never came home. They live in my heart and the hearts of many, and one day, we *will* know what happened…

BACK COVER

PSYCHIC DETECTIVE is a compelling insight into how a man referred to as "The World's Most Accurate Psychic" interprets spiritual clues about real-life crime and translates messages between the living and the dead. PSYCHIC DETECTIVE chronicles Scott Russell Hill's fascinating journey through the netherworld of cold cases and the clues he receives from the other side. Covering some of Australia and New Zealand's most notorious cases, Scott investigates the spiritual messages he receives and offers fresh insights into the often mysterious circumstances of the crime in question.

Cases include the Claremont serial killings, Karmein Chan and Mr. Cruel, the missing Beaumont Children, Queensland's Daniel Morcombe, and two of New Zealand's most baffling cases - Kirsa Jensen and Luana Williams.

Extraordinary and moving, this book gives a behind the scenes look at how Scott works as a PSYCHIC DETECTIVE.

Book Four in the CAUGHT BETWEEN TWO WORLDS series.

Made in the USA
Middletown, DE
04 September 2021